BACK IN THE

STONE AGE

The Natives of Central Australia

CHARLES CHEWINGS

Photographs by Frank Gillen

ETT IMPRINT
Exile Bay

This edition published by ETT Imprint, Exile Bay 2022

This book is copyright. Apart from any fair dealing for the purposes of private study, research, criticism or review, as permitted under the Copyright Act, no part may be reproduced by any process without written permission. Inquiries should be addressed to the publishers:

ETT IMPRINT
PO Box R1906
Royal Exchange NSW 1225 Australia

First published by Angus & Robertson in 1936

First electronic edition published by ETT Imprint in 2022

This edition copyright © Idriess Enterprises Pty Ltd, 2022

ISBN   978-1-922698-70-4   (col)
ISBN   978-1-922698-50-6   (ebk)

Cover: Walter Baldwin Spencer seated with the Aranda elders. Each of these men is the head of a particular totem group and together they directed the Engwura of 1896. Photograph by Frank Gillen

Cover and design by Tom Thompson

CONTENTS

Foreword 5
Introduction 9
1. EARLY MEMORIES OF THE RANGES 15
2. REMARKABLE FACULTIES AND PECULIAR HABITS 21
3. COMMUNISTS AND DEGENERATE LOAFERS 29
4. COPING WITH A DRY COUNTRY AND OTHER MATTERS 34
5. HEREDITARY TRAITS AND OTHER THINGS 43
6. TRAINING YOUNG FIGHTERS 53
7. THE MAGICIAN AND SUPERSTITION 58
8. PUNISHMENTS TO FIT THE CRIME 65
9. HOW THE WOMEN SETTLE THEIR LITTLE DIFFERENCES 73
10. BETROTHALS AND MARRIAGE CUSTOMS 80
11. LENDING AND EXCHANGE OF WIVES 84
12. CICATRICES AND MUTILATIONS 86
13. POLYGAMY. POLYANDRY AND MORAL MONSTROSITIES 90
14. WOMEN'S HARD LOT 92
15. EXPRESSIONS OF SORROW 96
16. THE SIGN LANGUAGE 99
17. THINGS THAT ARE PRIMITIVE 101
18. WHAT OF THEIR FUTURE? 109
Notes 116
Map 117

Aboriginal elder from the Arrernte tribe near Alice Springs, 1901.
He is an *Oknirabata*, a very wise old man.

Foreword

BACK IN THE STONE AGE is the fruit of nearly fifty years' acquaintance with the Central Australian natives. My experiences began in 1881-2. The Overland Telegraph Line had not long been completed. Central Australia, on the western side of the line, was largely an unknown land.

Ernest Giles, the explorer, in 1872 had followed the Finke River to the foot of the MacDonnell Ranges and, failing to get through the Finke Gorge, had turned westward and followed the southern side of the ranges until they fell away. Lack of water compelled him to turn south; there Lake Amadeus thwarted him; so he returned to the telegraph line. Colonel Warburton, in 1873, started west from Alice Springs. He skirted the north side of the MacDonnell Ranges to the Darwent Creek, then struck north-west into the desert; the party finished up by eating most of their camels. W. C. Gosse went westward from the telegraph line, about eighty miles north of Alice Springs, but soon made south, and passed through the western end of the MacDonnell Ranges, shortly after Warburton had left them.

All three explorers failed to reach the head of the Finke. Richard Egerton Warburton, upon his return from his father's ill-fated expedition, was sent by Grant and Stokes to try again to reach the head of the Finke. Believing the Finke Gorge (from Giles's account of it) to be impassable, he passed along the north side of the MacDonnells from Alice Springs and succeeded in reaching the heart of the ranges by following the Dashwood Creek to its source. From there he reached the head of the Finke.

Warburton formed the Glen Helen cattle station a mile or two north of the Finke Gorge, not long before I first went there in 1881. The Hermannsburg Mission Station, a few miles south of Glen Helen, had two or three small buildings erected. Parke and Walker's Ellery's Creek station had been recently shifted to Henbury, farther down the Finke. Mr McRae had been out to the George Gills Range, and had returned to Adelaide, and W. C. Gosse, after he had returned to Adelaide from his exploring trip, had been sent to fix a datum-point on the Finke for the pastoral leases applied for; but he had returned.

That embraces practically all the settlement on the upper Finke in 1881. The blacks were considered unsafe out from the stations and every one carried fire-arms. One could not be sure what their attitude would be. Along the telegraph line, south of Alice Springs, they were considered more trustworthy; but north of that place, right through to Darwin, everyone went armed.

In time the natives came to know that the whites would not harm them if they behaved themselves; the younger ones were given employment and soon learned to be useful. In after years I used them to do all sorts of. work on cattle stations, on the roads in the transport of stores with camels, on exploratory work, in gold- and wolfram-mining, in opening and in watering stock-routes, in mapping extensive tracts of country, and in domestic work. Some of the subject matter of this volume may seem to the reader so primitive as to be unthinkable. But the natives are very primitive beings, and what seems childish to us may be very important to them. I have tried to present the subject matter in such a way that "the man in the street" may understand the significance of it all. If I have done that, and at the same time made it interesting, I shall be content.

Here the reader will find, so far as I am able to show it, that side of the native he presents to all whom he comes in contact with.

During his pastorate at the Hermannsburg Mission Station, on the Finke River, the Rev. C. Strehlow collected many of the natives' traditions. The old men regard them as true; many of the details they contain are jealously guarded from the women and children. The natives' lives, to a great extent, are regulated by them, and their ceremonies find their inspiration in them. They comprise the major portion of what we know of their history. Their traditions throw little light on their distant past. These show that their ancestors lived where the natives now live; travelled about the same country; and hunted for their food in much the same way as today. While the teachings and acts related in the traditions may be mythical, there is no denying that they are universally and deeply implanted in the whole community. Nearly every water, creek, gorge, range, hill, or camping-place is named after some peculiarity, patronymic, or incident connected with the travels of some ancestor.

How the aborigines first came to Australia, and when, may never be known. Their distribution over the whole of the continent was probably an accomplished fact before the period of desiccation that now obtains over all the west-central portions; at any rate, before that period had reached the stage when rivers like the Finke, the Hanson and the Lander had ceased to flow, or the freshwater lakes had become saltpans, or the sand-dunes that extend over such huge areas were formed, or the giant marsupials had become extinct.

A mild drought is the normal state of Central Australia today. The present desiccation is thought to have followed on the heels of the last (Pleistocene) Ice Age.

It is doubtful if the natives, as a people, could survive in severe, protracted droughts if they practised any other than the communistic rule of sharing what food they are fortunate enough to catch. Like animals, they make no provision for tomorrow's food. All have the "wanderlust." Make no permanent shelter or camp, and camp any and everywhere. Their implements, their daily habits, their language, their conceptions of the origin of things, their cult, their social organization, and many other traits, all show that they are still in the Stone Age. Hence the title of this treatise.

The map is a locality map, to show where incidents mentioned in the text occurred. Routes of travel are not shown on the map because they form quite a network, and would only be confusing.

My cordial thanks are due to Professor Sir William Mitchell, K.C.M.G., Vice-Chancellor, and Professors J. B. Cleland and J. A. Fitzherbert, of the University of Adelaide for reading through the manuscript, and for goodly advice thereon; to Mr H. H. Finlayson, Hon. Curator of Mammals, South Australian Museum, for the photographs of Central Australian scenery; to the Hon. Minister of Education, and the Board of Governors of the Public Library, Museum and Art Gallery for the photographs of natives from the celebrated F. J. Gillen collection; and to Mr N. B. Tindale, B.Sc., Ethnologist of the South Australian Museum, for advice, In selecting them, All copyright in the illustrations is reserved.

Charles Chewings
Glen Osmond
South Australia
1936

Baldwin Spencer with Arrernte elders near Alice Springs photographed by Frank Gillen in 1896.

Carl Strehlow with elders of several tribes helping create a comparative Aboriginal dictionary in 1909.

Introduction

THE writer's first experiences of the natives of Central Australia was gained during a tour of inspection of a tract of country in the upper-Finke region in 1881-2, to determine whether it was suitable for cattle-raising.

The country had been leased from the Crown, and the title was good for a number of years provided one paid the annual rent in advance, and stocked up to a specified number per square mile within a given time. A peppercorn rental had been authorized for the first seven years to induce people to take up the huge vacant areas in the Northern Territory, and a mild "rush" to secure suitable land for pastoral pursuits was on. No special provisions for the care and preservation of the natives' rights in the natural waters and pastures were in force.

Central Australia was largely a *terra incognita* at that time. The Overland Telegraph Line, Adelaide to Darwin, was completed, and four or five cattle stations had been formed-three on or near the telegraph line and two on the Finke. The Hermannsburg Mission Station had been established on the Finke, and a new cattle station Glen Helen had quite recently been formed near the north end of the Finke Gorge, right in the heart of the MacDonnell Ranges. The road to Glen Helen from the mission station lay through the Finke Gorge, four miles long, with a waterhole stretching from side to side blocking its northern entrance. Of that, more anon .

As my land lay north of Glen Helen, to reach it I had to get through that waterhole; for high, steep, rocky ranges ran east and west of it for many miles. Deep water lay under the high rocks. But my black boy discovered a wadable sandspit, armpit deep, through the hole along which he led my two camels with much fear and trembling, for they were terror-stricken by the beetling rocks above.

The manager of Glen Helen kindly offered to pilot me to my land through the still higher ranges that lay to the north. Leaving the boy at the station, the manager rode one camel and I the other. We had to be cautious, for the natives out from the stations were unsafe in those days, and much given to cattle-killing. After passing over the Finke watershed, along which was some grand scenery of the bare granite type, but fearfully rough, we descended the northern side of the MacDonnells (a very steep-sided range) to the Burt Plain, just where the Halleem Creek leaves the range and runs through the open plain.

Numerous footprints on the sandy bed of the creek warned us of the presence of a large mob of natives in the vicinity; but we could neither see nor hear any. Being evening we had to camp. At dusk we heard great shouting that continued for a long while. All night long we kept a sharp look out for them, but they did not show themselves. Natives usually require time - a couple of days for palaver before they decide upon an attack. A wise precaution for a small party is to shift camp a few miles every day.

Having finished the inspection, Mr Alan Braden and I returned to Glen Helen without seeing any natives. Apparently they had all been summoned to Halleem Creek to perform certain ceremonies.

Part of my holding extended to the west and south-west of the mission block. Starting from the mission station with my black boy I travelled westward along the northern side of the Krichauff Range for a couple of days to inspect the country there. I saw no natives.

My boy narrowly escaped getting his skull smashed in with a blow from my camel's front foot. When he returned with the camels one morning he was covered with blood. I thought some natives must have beaten him about the head with a boomerang. He explained that my big bull camel, a nasty-tempered brute on occasion, had hit him with his front foot while being unhobbled. As all camelmen know, a camel can kick a smart blow with his hind foot; with the front foot he can bit a deadly blow either forwards or backwards, but not sideways. The boy evidently had got into a position where the animal could reach him, and had received a smashing blow over the head and face. Only the great strength of the native's skull saved his life; a European's skull must have been stove in.

When I returned to civilization I sold the camel to the Police Department. He was sent to the Peak, then a telegraph station. While there a black boy was sent one morning to bring in the camels. As the boy did not return with them a search was made. He was found dead and Battened out like a pancake; and the bull was found with blood about him. Tracks showed that the camel had caught and downed the boy and then dropped on him with his brisket. A camel's brisket is callous and hard. When fighting, if one can get the other bull down, he falls on his neck, then wriggles on to his head and smashes it.

There is a wide stretch (If range country lying to the south and south-west of the mission station, collectively known as the James Ranges. The only ways of access to parts of it are through the watercourses which the streams have eroded. One has therefore to travel sometimes through deep meandering trenches hedged in by precipitous red sandstone walls; at others through rough gorges, or along narrow plains bounded by steep rocky ranges on either side.

Charles Walker, one of the partners owning the Henbury cattle station, accompanied me to see my land in that direction. He rode on the rear camel, the boy being left at the station.

In two days from Henbury we reached the Palmer at its confluence with the Walker (named after my companion). As the Walker came from the direction in which I wished to go, we followed it and ten miles farther on found that it ran through a narrow pass, with high ranges on either side. The creek-bed, occupying nearly the full width of the pass, was filled with high reeds and deep waterholes. By going carefully along the side, close against the towering wall of rock, we got through safely, and then found we were in a narrow plain, bounded by steep ranges.

A mile or so east of the pass the ranges coalesced and the plain ended there; to the westward it widened and the ranges fell apart a little, but looked quite impassable. Eight or nine miles off a steep-sided range, as high as the other two, showed up in the middle of the plain. Following the creek, we found it came from the direction of the valley between the middle and the north range, which latter was getting lower and appeared to terminate in a plain. Around this the middle range curved and formed a high, precipitous, and intensely red wall of rock, with no visible opening in it anywhere.

Before we reached the end of the north range we saw the smokes of a large camp of natives on our right, and four or five miles farther on we surprised a woman and two or three children. The woman was paralysed with fright and stood still, but the children hid themselves. After a while the woman began to regain her wits and climbed a tree, where she broke off a stiff bough, and made ready to defend herself.

Without putting the camels down we passed on and at dusk made camp on an open spot near the creek. Usually the creek was lined with a thick border of *Acacia* and *Eucalyptus*, and the banks rather steep. Its course through the plain was tortuous. A drizzling rain fell all night long. We feared that the creek might come down in flood, and block our return passage through the pass. Being anxious about the natives, too, breakfast was eaten before dawn, and we started back along our out-going tracks as day was breaking.

We had not gone more than a mile when we had to cross the creek. The banks were rather steep and on the opposite side was an open space right on our road with thick Acacias around it. Crossing the creek, we ascended the bank and were just entering the open space when, as if by magic, we were confronted by fifty or more men in a half-circle with their spears poised ready to throw. I whispered to my companion to get his revolver ready, unbuckled my rifle and, without stopping the camels, covered the leader but did not fire.

Evidently they had heard of fire-arms, for they dropped their spears and vanished as mysteriously as they had appeared. It was a tense moment, for they were easily within throwing distance, and with so many ours was a poor chance. The rain all night had compelled them to hug their fires until daylight. otherwise they probably would have speared us before we left camp. We did not touch their spears but hastened on to get through the pass before a flood overtook us.

In due course we arrived at Henbury, and soon afterwards I left for Adelaide.

It will be seen from the foregoing that the natives were still in their pristine state fifty-four years ago when the writer first went among them. Since then, all have been steadily if unconsciously absorbing European customs, habits, speech, ideas, and ways; the leaven has reached and is affecting even those who still live far from any European settlement. The white man's ways are a much discussed subject, not without ridicule among them.

The time for stocking the country with cattle soon came round, and April 1885 found me again on the upper Finke. As there were no other maps of the country I held than those showing the routes of the explorers, Giles, Gosse, and Warburton, it was necessary for me to travel all over the country to locate any waters that promised to be of service when the stock we had taken there increased in numbers. For this purpose I took a string of eight camels and, as the number and disposition of the natives one might meet was an unknown quantity, I also took two white men and one black boy.

There were then many more natives in the ranges than there are to-day, and it was interesting to note the effect the sudden appearance of our caravan made upon the many groups we came across. I well remember coming upon about a dozen men, women, and children one day in the Mount Zeil locality; they were so engrossed with what they were hunting that they neither saw us, nor beard the camels until we were right upon them. The men dropped their spears, the women their *pittjis* and all they held, and fled with the children for high grass that grew in a watercourse near by. Upon reaching it they bent low and disappeared from view. We called to them, and the boy did likewise, but no sight or sound of any of them could we get. How they hid themselves so well in the grass was a mystery. Without touching their belongings we proceeded on our way.

On several occasions while we were following the creek channels through the precipitous-sided ranges they would, upon catching sight of us, clamber up the rocks so high that they appeared very small; rarely one could see them, they dodged so cleverly behind the rocks. They refused to answer or come down. One day we surprised a rather large mob of lubras and children fishing at a place called Middletons Ponds. In a flash they had climbed the rocks and disappeared. We often surprised small groups of lubras with children. If no cover was near they would stand and stare as if paralysed; it was most difficult to get them to talk. It has since occurred to me that it might have been the sight of the camels that scared them so.

As our wandering lasted several months, and no harm came to them through us, they became less shy, and would remain while we paid a visit to their camps to make presents of a little food or tobacco. By degrees friendly relations were established.

Arrernte woman with child, *pittji* on her head and carrying a digging stick (detail). Alice Springs, 1896.

Members of the Horn Expedition, Alice Springs 1894.

Chance and wagon leaving Oodnadatta, 1901.

I

EARLY MEMORIES OF THE RANGES

I SHALL never forget the rapture with which I gazed for the first time on many of those picturesque, red, steep walls of sandstone rock that hemmed us in as we threaded our way through the ranges. There was, I repeat, no other way but through the creeks and passes. The rocky walls seemed to be devoid of soil; but high up there were white-barked gum-trees with crooked stems, clumps of native figs, and zamia palms all growing out of crevices in the bare rocks. How they got sufficient nutriment to exist on is a mystery.

Occasionally we would come upon small groups of natives composed of one or two families camped by a waterhole or spring. If we passed a camp in the day-time they would be out foraging for food; the men on the ranges, the women and children on the flats. The women seemed to find edible leaves on many shrubs, for they picked and ate as they went along.

All the women and most of the young girls carried wooden trays, or *pittjis*, mostly of the shallow variety and twice to three times as long as they were broad - a shape convenient to carry on the hip under the arm. Women with infants carried them in outsized trays, and when they were digging for yams, bulbs, yelka, lizards, rats and honey-ants, the tray with the child in was placed in the shade nearby and a small girl had charge of it with a twig to brush the flies off.

How those women would dig! Hour after hour they kept at it, loosening the earth with their yam-sticks, and throwing it back with a small hardwood tray. When in camp this tray is put to several uses: it is a shovel to shift hot ashes with which to cook the rats and lizards. If seeds require roasting to make them grind better, or yelka-bulbs peeling, they are placed in this tray and covered with: hot ashes; then the tray is rotated until the seeds. or bulbs are partially roasted; the winnowing of the ashes from the seed follows.

Probably there are no more expert winnowers with dishes, anywhere, than the native women of Central Australia. After many years' practice in testing the values of gold ores one gets fairly expert at "panning off," that is, separating the gangue from the gold; but I have never yet seen a gold-washer that could clean and separate seeds like the native women. I have often seen the women scraping up the rings of grass-seeds and chaff that a certain kind of ant gathers and places around the entrance to the nest - for future use. The women would place all in a *pittji*, rub loose the matted mass of sand, sticks, chaff and seed, then by using two or three trays for winnowing, and occasional blowings with the mouth, the seed would be cleaned.

A set of wooden trays is of more value to a native woman than a completely furnished kitchen, pantry, and wash-house is to a European housewife. With these trays they can gather many kinds of seeds, sufficient for their requirements; with them they are able to clean the seeds ready for grinding. As they grind the seed they dampen it by spraying water from the mouth; the porridge-like mass is then scraped off into a tray, the only vessel they have to hold it.

No sooner do they reach their camping-place after hunting than the grinding of seeds starts.

A species of *Acacia* lines the banks of most of the watercourses in Central Australia=-or did before the white man's stock destroyed the bushes. These formerly yielded large quantities of seed at certain seasons of the year. The seeds are hard, black, and tough. The native women gather them in large quantities in their *pittjis*, warm them on hot stones or in hot ashes, then crack them and grind them between two stones, at the same time moistening the meal with water to the consistency of pea soup, which in appearance it somewhat resembles. As just stated, the water is squirted from the mouth of the woman while grinding the grain.

From time to time the soup is. pushed off the nether millstone into a shallow *pittji* until enough has been prepared. This is taken upon the two front fingers - or rather the fingers are besmeared through dipping them into it. They are then drawn across the tongue, in the way children eat "lick stick." This is a staple food with them when Acacia-seeds are "in." As no thought :is taken for the future, when Acacia-seeds are "out" they do without them, not having laid any in store. They follow the same improvident rule with all other kinds of seeds they may gather, and all other food.

The succulent plant, munyeroo, also yields quantities of edible seeds that they treat in the same way.

At all the main camps and waters in Central Australia grinding-stones may be seen. The nether millstone is a flat stone, mostly of quartzite or sandstone, and the upper a waterworn oval pebble, twice or three times the size of a cricket ball. The latter is first used to crack the seeds, a few at a time, and then, when grinding, the wrist is moved up and down in a switchback style. at which the lubras are highly skilled. I regret not having a snapshot of one old man's face I saw after he had finished a meal of Acacia-seed soup at Tempe Downs station. It resembled the snout of a pig after eating pollard-squash from a trough more than anything else I can think of.

Grinding seeds is a tedious game.

All rats, lizards, snakes, or grubs collected by the women are also cooked in the ashes. The women cook the small fry, and the men the large.

Natives of mature years invariably have their teeth well worn down. This is through having to masticate food with much sand in it. They are not fastidious about a little sand on their food. If a piece of meat they are eating happens to fall in the sand they either hit it against something to knock the sand off, or hold it up with the finger and thumb of the left hand and give it a flick with the thumb and finger of the right hand. When the husband has eaten as much as he wants off a bone he throws it over his shoulder in the direction of his wife and children. They just pick it up, knock the sand off and eat as if nothing unusual had happened

To make string they pull the hair and fur out of animals they catch, and squeeze them into a ball. This they draw out and, with the aid of two sticks* tied like the cross of a kite, twist it into yarn and wind it on the sticks at the same time. This is again twisted on the bare thigh by the women and made into strong string. Human hair is twisted into string also. From this string cord necklaces, cord headlaces, headbands, armbands, waistbands, and other articles are made, and worn as in the illustrations. The hair of a dead person is cut off before burial and twisted up for specific purposes.
The love for a fire close by is present in all natives.

They seem to be lost without a fire. They tended their fires most meticulously, and always more than one carried a fire-stick when out hunting. That, of course, was before they had learned to beg matches from the whites. How to make fire by rubbing two pieces of wood together has apparently always been known by the natives. But that means exertion. To keep a fire going is easier than making it by friction.

The native does much sitting on the ground. He does not sprawl his legs about as every European finds it necessary to do. No European could sit in the position the native assumes without experiencing great discomfort; and it is doubtful, unless he happened to be double-jointed, whether he could get his legs into the position the native finds most comfortable.

The knee of the native is very accommodating; it is like the knee-joint of a camel. When a native sits on the ground his body is erect on the fundamental part of him, his knees are straight in front, and owing to his natural deficiency of muscle and flesh on the under lower thigh and calf, the leg from the knee down can lie flat against the thigh with the foot turned either inwards or outwards. If inwards the heel is tucked right in the crutch, or fork, or the entire foot can be sat upon, or the foot may be turned toe out-

---

* The long stick is sharpened at one end so that it can be stood in the ground.

wards and rest flat on the ground just outside the thigh. Hour after hour both men and women sit with their legs doubled under them in this way. When they do get up sweat marks, like those a collar leaves on a horse, cover the under part of the knee, the under thigh and the calf.

For convenient sitting on my camp-sheet or tarpaulin, I tried to acquire the art of doubling my legs under me in true native fashion, but failed dismally. The positions appear to be quite impossible to Europeans unless they happen to be double-jointed all round.

The superior workmanship of native weapons, and the wooden trays and troughs of the women, impressed me. Only the men made these things. The trays, troughs, and shields were mostly made from the light, soft wood of that beautiful drooping willow-like tree commonly known as Stuart's bean-tree (*Erythrina vespertilio*); the spears and spear-throwers were made from harder woods. A stone axe was used to cut the tree down and roughly fashion the article; all else had to be done with a bit of flint set on the end of a short weighty stick.

With this primitive tool they would sit close to their little fire hour after hour and chip, chip, chip away. Occasionally a slight halt was necessary while the resin that held the flint in position was warmed at the fire to soften. it for renewal of the flint, or to turn it to a fresh cutting-edge. Five or ten minutes sufficed for this and to cool the cement, then at it they would go again, both legs. tucked under in the way I have described.

The spinifex resin, to which reference is made in Chapter 4, must be a very powerful adhesive, and very tough to stand the jarring. It sets like cement. How they would have got along without this resin I do not. know, for they could not have made their weapons and trays without some tool with a cutting-edge. They used the resin with animal sinews to join their spears, to fix a barb in their spears, to fix the blunt barb on one end of' the spear-thrower, and a flint in the other end. They used the latter as a knife to cut up an animal, if they had no stone knife, or to trim up their spears.

Spinifex gum, as it is usually called, is a most useful commodity; rarely can one find a native without a piece of it. It is an article of barter: one of the few things. a native really required in former time to enable him to live.

It has been remarked that the whites brought to the natives their diseases. They may have brought some, but not all. There was a disease, very widespread, that they called *yerakintja* or *irkintja*. While mapping in the country, near one of my camps at the head of the Palmer, a dozen or more men were camped nearby. Before starting on the day's journey I walked over to them to make a little present of tobacco. As I approached they all stood in a row. One poor unfortunate was a mass of sores right round him, and extending from his armpits to the crutch. Flies were about him like a swarm of bees; but the others did not seem to fear them or shun him in any way not-withstanding his loathsome appearance. In after years many instances of diseased natives came under my notice, some of whom doubtless contracted their diseases either primarily or secondarily from the whites. But I agree with Strehlow that diseases were amongst the natives before ever they came in contact with the whites, ones for which they had their own specific remedies.

Diseased natives employed by whites were given curatives. They always approached me with confidence, and other whites, I know, in the same spirit.

Two Aranda women with a baby, Alice Springs 1895.

Aranda man named Twairira, of the *Echunpu* (Lizard) totem.
Alice Springs, 1896.

2

REMARKABLE FACULTIES AND PECULIAR HABITS

I HAD not been long among the natives of Central Australia before I realized that, not-withstanding their backward state in many directions, they possess very remarkable faculties of observation, and good reasoning powers, more particularly as regards the means whereby they subsist. They know the habits of every living thing around them, great or small. Captain S. A. White has expressed the opinion that they are, in this respect, the -most competent naturalists that ever were, or ever will be. With the sure knowledge that they can find food when they go forth to hunt tomorrow, they make the best and most of the present.

And so we find them a happy-go-lucky people, merry and fond of amusement, with a keen sense of the ridiculous. Their habits and customs are largely the result of their environment. They must have taken many generations to spread over the entire continent, and longer still to acquire their present status and condition. They possess no means of transporting food and water other than by carrying them in skins or wooden troughs.

Their distribution was surely accomplished prior to the great desiccation that now obtains over all the central and western-central portions of the continent. One can hardly conceive of them pushing out into, and settling in Gibson's, Victoria, and Simpson's deserts, in their present forbidding state. And yet, in all probability, there is not one square mile in all Australia - with the possible exception of portions of the Nullarbor Plain that they did not know, and periodically hunt over, prior to the advent of the whites. The lack of water did not deter them, for they knew which roots to dig up and drain water from.

Michael Terry has recently recorded an instance of a small party of natives that he had followed nearly to Mount. Farewell, not far from the Western Australian border in order to locate their watering-place. When he overtook them they had then been four days in warm weather without a drink. They were not carrying anything to hold water, nor were they in any hurry to go to a supply. They quenched their thirst with the moisture from yams.

Nomadic instincts they all possess, the outcome probably of having had to hunt for food since their Australian existence began. They store no food; take no thought for the morrow; eat everything they catch soon after it is caught, and pride themselves on the quantity they can eat.

The principal food of the emaciated beings we find dwelling in the driest and sandiest parts of the interior are snakes, lizards, berries, leaves of shrubs, seeds of Acacia, munyeroo and parakeelia-seeds, grass-seeds, yams, mulga apples, rats, and grubs that at certain seasons of the year are found in the roots and on the leaves of trees and bushes - largely of *Acacia* species. They rarely get a kangaroo, wallaby, or emu in those desolate regions.

I have sometimes wondered why they do not shift to more pleasant surroundings; but having no sense of the beautiful, a desert probably makes as happy a home for them as an elysium. True, a cool, shady retreat in the blazing heat appeals to the natives, or a cosy spot to camp in when the frosty nights of winter make them bundle together, like a litter of little pigs. But where plenty of food is to be found, that spot to them is heavenly, provided water to slake their thirst is within reach.

Stony or spinifex country, or parts thickly bestrewn with bindi-eyes (three-cornered jacks) or spiky grass-seeds, that make their feet sore when hunting or travelling, are to them an abomination. One often sees the native trail composed of only a single individual's tracks for those that follow tread on his tracks to avoid the burrs. Not-withstanding the leathery soles of their feet the burrs often penetrate, break off, and bring lameness.

Their dominant likes and dislikes may briefly be summed up in the words "appetite" and "comfort" and their implications. Conversation largely keeps to those subjects.

The naming of places has usually some significance with natives. A hill, a water, or a watercourse may be helpful as landmarks or drinking-places in their journeyings; consequently they bear a name, often a name given to commemorate some incident in the life of some apocryphal ancestor. Objects that serve no useful purpose to them will have no name. It has often been a puzzle to travellers how to obtain the native name of some feature of interest. To the native that object may have no interest, and consequently was never named; or if it has, the name, being so rarely used, is only known to the old men, who are the geographers of the tribe.

"Locality" is a largely developed sense in all natives. From earliest youth the perception and reasoning faculties are trained for the dual purpose of getting about the country, and tracking for food everything that creeps or walks. In every native, in some much more than in others, hereditary traits have been developed through many generations, and thereby specialized. In winter, when the lizards and snakes are hibernating, the natives find it difficult to obtain much flesh food, but as soon as the spring heat calls forth the reptiles, and they in their wanderings leave tracks, the native, through his perfected accomplishment of tracking, unerringly runs his prey to its hiding.

For the following of trails by scent their mongrel, or pure dingo, dogs are of great service, and consequently are much prized. They appear to rank with the children in value, and are indulged as bedmates. If food is plentiful, the worst parts of game are cast to the dogs; if scarce, the dogs have to go hungry.

The natives themselves will gather bits of cow-hide, soak and toast them, pound them up and eat the product. When a severe drought is on they and their dogs endure great privation. If children are born they are not reared; the nurse in attendance dispatches them and the mother shows no sorrow or regret. I know of an instance where the mother, being alone, did the deed herself; she did not, however, eat the child, as some are reported to have done when on the verge of starvation.

In his primitive state the Australian native is indescribably filthy. The only time he indulges in a bath is in the heat of summer, when he swims in the nearest waterhole to cool himself - never with the object of cleanliness. Only in wet weather do the natives think of making wurleys, or any other protection from inclement weather. They usually seek the shelter of caves or overhanging rocks when it rains; but, being superstitious, they will not venture near some places.

Natives never make a bed, but scratch out a shallow hole or hollow which they call a camp-hole - *tmara junta*. This resembles the hole a kangaroo scratches to lie down in. If the ground be damp they make a fire on a convenient spot, and later scrape the ashes away and sleep where the fire has been. Their usual custom is to fix the camp in the shelter afforded by some bush or rock, or in the bed of a creek, dig the necessary *junta*, and lie on the bare ground, with a small fire on either side to keep warm. If very cold a third fire is made at the feet. One frequently sees a long row of sleep-holes in a straight. line, with the ashes of fires between each. They huddle together, two in a hole, with the small children in addition, their only covering being the sky above.

When away from civilization for any length of time, the station blacks, both men and women, discard all clothing and hunt naked, like the wild ones. Upon returning they don the discarded clothes - if they were provident enough to hide them. Now, one rarely sees unclothed natives near the telegraph line, but away from it their primitive condition of nudity is the normal state.

Unlike the natives of the southern and eastern coastal regions, the Central Australian natives make no clothing of any kind from skins or fibre, and the climate is such that they need none. True, in winter they suffer from the cold, especially the biting cold winds which are sometimes terrible; but with the open-air life and warm weather returning, they throw their colds and other ailments off quickly if unclothed; if clothed, the reverse appears to be the case. A native boy in employment will almost invariably strip off his coat, shirt, and trousers before going to sleep, whether he has a blanket or not. All, both male and female, prefer to sleep naked between fires, but, if they have a blanket, will pull it over them. In the cold winter nights - and the winter nights are bitterly cold there - they hug the fires so closely that in turning they get badly burned at times. Frequently one sees great scars on their arms and legs from this cause.

For shade in the summer a few leafy branches are thrown upon a slanting bush. This thickens the shade and, as the sun moves round, the native shifts position.

The customary method of greeting is quite formal. Upon arrival at a camp a native does not go up and introduce himself, or look at those he has come to see. He stops some distance away and, squatting on the ground, pretends to be quite oblivious of them and his surroundings. They, in turn, also look everywhere but at him. Some minutes later one of the camp natives makes a casual remark, possibly about the weather, or puts a question, say, the condition of a water, or the road; then the visitor is invited to draw near, and conversation becomes general. Or a messenger-native may stand some distance from the camp, hold his spears upright on the ground with points upwards, and place the sole of one foot above the knee of the other leg. In that attitude he awaits the arrival of someone from the camp to invite him in. Once in, his status as regards totem and class are soon ascertained, and he becomes the guest of his own fraternity.

Whenever they approached my camp (most of them knew me by sight, or repute) they would say "*ngwarla unti*" (give me tobacco) or "*ngieela*" (I am hungry), or "*munns unti*" (give me food). Their troubles are largely about food; but through habit they can exist on little. When it is obtainable they eat, like animals, until they can eat no more. A sleep follows; then they eat again *ad nauseam* and become quite distended. When all is eaten they wait until hungry before looking for more.

As a rule the natives are fairly honest. But knives and tomahawks are a great temptation; tobacco is quite irresistible to those who have tasted it; and flour, meat, tea, and sugar can hardly be resisted.

In the early days (1881-2) when old Glen Helen station was first formed, the manager was put to his wit's end to know how the beef disappeared from the meat-house so quickly; watch-dogs were kept, and the two or three natives who assisted in the household duties were well and regularly fed, as also were the boys who assisted with the stock. All hands were told of this, and cautioned with many threats. All to no purpose, the beef kept on disappearing. At last things grew so serious that strategy had to be resorted to, seeing that no tracks were found whereby the culprits could be identified.

The station stood on the bank of the Ormiston, one of the chief upper tributaries of the Finke River, in the heart of the highest and ruggedest part of the MacDonnell Ranges, where the Finke - that largest of Central Australian watercourses - takes its rise. Without being seen the natives could lie concealed in the rocks all day, then steal along the sandy bed of the Ormiston to the station under cover of the bank any night without being detected. This they did most nights. Having an accomplice at the station to unfasten the meat-house door after the cook had, as he thought, securely fastened it on retiring to rest at night, certain old women, with their feet padded, made regular visits to the meat-house, and invariably took the under pieces of meat that had been salted down from the last slaughtering.

One night the household natives were all taken into safe custody, and a watch was kept. In the early morning, long before daybreak, the manager, who had concealed himself in the meat-house, heard the door open. Two women stole softly in, stood stock still for some time listening, then started to remove the meat. They carefully avoided disturbing the surface pieces. While thus engaged, the manager gently closed the door and stood against it. When they had placed the desired quantity in their wooden trays, they turned softly and, the night being pitch-dark, felt for the door - and found weals of skin developing all over their bodies in a remarkably short space of time.

The beef lasted longer after that.

A bucking horse, a ferocious bullock, or a humorous episode will send them into roars of laughter. I have seen them laugh till the tears ran down their cheeks. Many years ago a police inspector journeyed far inland to see his police officers. At Charlotte Waters was a mounted constable who had been stationed in that district for many years. When he first went there he was a fine, strapping, well-proportioned young man. Being of careful, saving habits he had packed away his regimentals carefully, they being unnecessary in such an out-of-the-way place, and there they remained. The climate, good food, and little exercise agreed with the trooper, and he put on much condition.

The inspector, wishing to know whether his officers were keeping up practice in sword exercise, and knowing that formerly this officer was an adept at the art, ordered him to don his uniform and give an exhibition. With considerable difficulty the constable got into his long-disused suit. All went well until those exercises requiring greater freedom came on, when a tear occurred here, and buttons flew off there!

Some of the onlookers were station natives. These, without exception, never moved a lip or a hair during the exhibition; but when it was over a native lad got to work with a piece of chalk. On the walls of the house and on the tanks the whole proceedings were depicted in a series of sketches. The constable was there, sword in hand, with abnormal drop-chest development, the perspiration streaming from him, rips and tears in his regimentals, and buttons flying in all directions; the agony on his face was indescribable.

Some of the natives undoubtedly possessed drawing ability. My working boys often drew animals, reptiles, and men and women in humorous attitudes and with speaking facial expressions, on the sides of the large tanks for watering stock at the wells along the telegraph line. I knew well a boy who ran the mails from Alice Springs to Burt Well during my stay at that place. He surprised me on many occasions by his drawings, of which he was - and justifiably - very proud. He had the art in him; he only needed tuition.

Anything having tangible existence the natives grasp readily enough; but on things abstruse, or existing in the mind only, they seem unable to concentrate. And yet they must have good reasoning ability to be so proficient as trackers; for perception alone - quite a remarkable feature with them - will not make a good tracker. From what they see they deduce where the animal, or man, is making for, and that carries them over parts and places where no tracks are visible. Probably more remarkable still is their ability to tell how old a track is, and to whom or what it belongs. They know the track of everything they have to do with, be it man, woman, child, or beast. And you cannot deceive them in this matter for they have observed certain peculiarities and reasoned them to finality.

Natives are naturally indisposed to labour or physical exertion, and lack mental activity. They have mental capability, but beyond their ordinary occupations it is difficult to get them to reflect and to think along lines we are accustomed to. They apparently experience no regrets for the pain they may have caused in a fit of anger, or through neglect. How often have I found them out in giving the animals only half a drink because they were too lazy to draw sufficient water to satisfy them!

They are good mimics, and can imitate the peculiar mode of speech or habits of anyone or anything. This ability is raised to a fine art by those who demonstrate the incidents contained in certain of their ceremonies that illustrate the lives and actions of their totem-fore-fathers.

Natives in their camp-life, their search for food, and in travels generally of necessity meet each other in all sorts of places. Some whom they meet belong to groups that are blood or tribal relatives; others belong to groups that etiquette permits friendly speech with at a distance; others again to groups that are strictly taboo to one another. Not-withstanding that they go about nude, they always practise a certain decorum, the two sexes keeping ten or fifteen yards apart when they meet; if nearer approach is necessary, they keep their backs to one another, or the women step quickly aside. Their behaviour to one another is regulated by custom, and is as orderly as our own.

In addition to the above there are prearranged meetings, at recognized depots, between sections of the same tribe who live far apart, or with a friendly neighbouring tribe. These have no cult significance, being for barter or exchange of commodities that occur, or can be made, in certain parts of the country and not in others. For example, red ochre is obtainable on the south side of Levis Range, and soft-wood trays are made where Stuart's bean-tree (*Erythrina vespertilio*) grows, in and north of the MacDonnell Ranges. The exchanges, for the most part, take place in weapons, implements, personal decoration commodities, and such like. Tjoritja (Alice Springs) is one of these exchange depots. The Anglepole waterhole, from which Oodnadatta takes its name, is another.

Strehlow has pointed out that Oodnadatta is a corruption of Utnadata - that being the name of the Anglepole waterhole. The meaning of Utnadata is "the flowers of the mulga-tree."

An Arrernte Tjitjingalla ceremony. Alice Springs, 1901.

Aboriginal workers. Alice Springs, April 1901.

3

COMMUNISTS AND DEGENERATE LOAFERS

THE natives, in their family groups, and to a considerable extent as a community also, are true communists as regards food. It is difficult to see how they could get along in any other way, for when food is scarce and luck is against a hunter, he may go for days without catching anything. The sharing of food is drilled into the children from earliest infancy; both sexes are taught the lesson until it is deeply ingrained. Later they are taught to whom food must first be given, and to whom next and next. None goes without altogether, even if the portion is very small.

Every man, woman, boy, or girl in the employ of a European is in honour bound to put aside a portion of every meal for relatives (blood or tribal) or friends if they be camped near. The boys may swear a dying oath that they have eaten the lot, and that they never give any away; but they are not to be believed in this matter. I am fully persuaded that if a youth persisted in ignoring his superiors they would make an end of him at the first opportunity. But the boys never forget to lay some aside for friend or relative and if possible carry it to them, or place it in some prearranged spot.

This tribal duty is reciprocal: today it is A's turn to be in work and receiving food; tomorrow it will be B's; so A must give to B today, and B to A tomorrow. All share in what comes to hand, but not share and share alike. The old men see to it that they get not only the choice morsels but the lion's share.

In their native state they are diligent, enterprising hunters; but when they taste the white man's food, and find how easy it is to live on those who happen to be in work, whether male or female, the enterprising hunter degenerates into a cadger or sponger, develops indolent habits, concocts schemes for killing cattle, or other devilment, and "the last state of that man is worse than the first. " The following is an instance of how this class of native goes to work:

The season was a dry one when a large boiler for the stamper-battery at a place called Winnecke, in the MacDonnell Ranges, was being conveyed thither. The horses had to be-taken to the Francis Well, some seventy-eight miles south of Alice Springs, to be spelled for some weeks. At the end of that time, having secured other horses from an adjoining station to replace those that were not fit to work, and being unable to obtain good black boys for the purpose, we engaged two trustworthy women.

Women are called lubras or *aragutja*, if matured; if young, *araweja uiunka*, i.e. woman young; *kwea* is a girl.

The lubras undertook to draw water for the horses while we were away, some three or four weeks. Rations were weighed out to them, and strict instructions given that only a certain proportion was to be used each day. At the end of eight days I returned to see how the horses were doing. During that time several spongers had come on the scene and demanded that they be fed. The lubras had no choice, and all the rations were gone. A travelling. caravan of camels happened to be passing, so I purchased a duplicate quantity of rations and gave strict instructions as before. No sooner was my back turned than the spongers came back, and, long before the time was up, the rations were all gone, and the lubras had to obtain their food as best they could. For a week or ten days they nearly starved.

While camped on the Hanson Creek at its nearest point to Central Mount Stuart, I was interested in watching two lads of our party wandering about the sandy bed of the creek. Every now and again they would go down on their knees, with one hand dig a hole arm-deep, then bring up a much inflated frog, three inches long or more. With a squeeze the frog lost the water that inflated it and it was thrust inside the lad's shirt, to keep company with many more.

The lads assured me that when on a long dry stage a native comes across a creek where frogs are to be had, and he is thirsty, be promptly digs them up and squeezes down his throat the water they hold.

The Hanson at that time had no known water either on the surface or in the sand near our camp, but a sprinkling rain a day or two previously had brought the frogs to the surface; a small round spot of disturbed sand indicated to the boys where to dig. When they had dug up enough they threw them on the fire and warmed them a little. Then with the assistance of their teeth they were dismembered; the fleshy parts eaten, and the refuse cast over the shoulder, or to one side. One frog quickly followed another until all were gone. The sight was nauseating.

The boys then turned their attention to a thick clump of bushes, a species of Acacia (*A. Kempeana*) close by, and with yam-sticks began digging up the roots and breaking them in pieces. They were extracting cream coloured grubs, called by the natives *yappa*. When they had obtained enough, the grubs were laid in hot ashes and rolled over and over for a minute or two, the head was then gripped by the nails of forefinger and thumb, the tail part and body placed in the mouth, bitten off close to the head, and eaten. The natives often eat them without warming them. But they will not eat many at one time if uncooked. Possibly the food is too rich.

I have often seen the boys eat raw the great brown moth-like cicadas found on the gum-trees (*Eucalyptus rostrata*) along the watercourses. They remove the wings and legs, hold the head as above described, place the tail part in the mouth and bite off the head. A bushman I had in the party used to eat the grubs like the natives, when cooked, and his verdict was:

"They are as rich as cream, and quite as nice."

Around Central Mount Stuart the natives at a certain time of the year largely subsist on these grubs; the same may be said of many other localities where *Acacia Kempeana* grows plentifully. The natives prod the ground around the stem of the bush with the point of a yam-stick, and by the sound are able to detect the spot near which a grub-holding root lies below. A few digs with the yam-stick reveal the root, the yam-stick is thrust under it, and the root is broken by leverage in the weakest spot - just where the juicy morsel lies. The grub is placed in the wooden tray, and so the search goes on hour after hour for the *wittjetti* or *tjappa* insect larva. Both the *wittjetti* and the cicadas grow to the size of the third finger of a man's hand, in some cages even larger. They are regarded as delicacies.

On one occasion while we were camped at the Francis Well a mob of natives were seen gathering in great numbers a green caterpillar, two to three inches long, and thicker than a lead pencil in girth. They were in countless numbers, and travelling on a broad front across a patch of green grass several acres in extent. Very voracious, they ate day and night, clearing the grass as they advanced. The native women as they gathered them pulled their heads off, held them by the tail-end, and emptied them by drawing finger and thumb downwards. The remainder was then dried in hot ashes and eaten or placed in a string bag dry. Later they were pounded lightly between stones, kneaded into a paste, and baked on the coals.

While living on these caterpillars, the natives emit a most disagreeable odour.

In his primitive state the native has no pockets in his clothes. This may not at first strike one; but when one sees grubs entangled in and dangling from the hair of his head, like ringlets of a former fashion, or dangling from the hair-cord all natives wear around the waist - the heads only being tucked under the girdle - the fact is forced upon one's attention.

The natives drink water as they find it - excepting when they sweeten it by soaking in it certain honey-holding flowers or the sweet wafer-like substance found on the leaves of some of the Eucalypts, or by dissolving in it the gum from certain Acacias. They are very observant of the indications of the presence of water at shallow depth, as their gnamma-hole[1] waters show. But they are not wholly dependent on ground water. Elsewhere mention has been made of natives existing for indefinite periods on the moisture contained in yams. They also obtain water from mallee-roots, and from the roots of the kurrajong (*ngalta*) tree. They run the roots out by uncovering them for some distance from the butt, break them in short lengths, place them upright (big end down) in a *pittji*, and the water draws out. It is said they also get water by tapping the grass-trees (*Xanthorroea*). But I have never witnessed that.

As regards food generally, anything that is edible, tough or tender, in either the vegetable or animal kingdom "goes down." Their staple food however consists of seeds which the lubras gather from grasses, plants, and bushes.[2] Animals, lizards, snakes, birds, and fishes - anything that is big enough to be worthwhile (with very few exceptions) is eaten. Rabbits and domestic cats, since they have spread over the interior, have been added to the bill of fare.

The fur, or hair, of animals if not required for making string is singed off first in a blazing fire, and then the charred hair is well rubbed off with the hands. They are very particular about this.

All flesh, or fish, is cooked in hot ashes, i.e. partially cooked only; the native prefers his meat nearly raw.

Then there are certain bulbs, roots of rushes, and yams. Many acres of ground by the watercourses are dug over in gathering the small shallot-like bulbs, called yelka (*Cyperus rotundus*). To remove the outer skins the bulbs are dried by shaking them to and fro mixed with hot ashes in a *pittji*. In small lots the ashes are then blown away from the bulbs by the mouth; rubbing them together and blowing the husks away completes the process. They are either eaten in that state, or rubbed to a powder and eaten as porridge.

Central Australia must be about the poorest place on earth for native fruits. The native peach is perhaps the best, but localities in which many trees grow are few. In rocky ground in the ranges the native orange (*Capparis nummularia*) is common enough. They call it *mbultjita*. It has great attraction for a white butterfly. These lay their eggs, and the grubs that hatch from them spoil what would otherwise be an edible fruit. There are so-called plums, a kind of gooseberry, and a sort of blackberry, all of which the natives are fond of - but all poor fruit from the European's standpoint.

Anything sweet the natives will expend time and labour to get. The so-called "sugar-bag," i.e. a hive of the small stingless bee, they will spend hours in chopping out of a hollow tree, and will dig deep holes to get the honey-ant. The white wafer-like sugary secretion with which a small lerp insect covers itself on the leaves of certain Eucalypts, they collect and eat. They also steep honey-holding flowers in water, express the juice, and drink the water. A little mosquito-like insect collects honey in the knobs of bloodwood-trees, of this also they are very fond. They call it *iwunji-wunja* - little black mosquito.

(The name is a lesson in linguistics: *iwultja*, or *uwinga*, means mosquito, and the native's way of expressing anything in diminutive form is to repeat the word, which then translates "mosquito-mosquito.")

They are fond of fish. Floods wash the fish out of deep waterholes into shallower ones, or the waters may become shallow by drying up. The fish are often speared with a short light spear while the fisherman stands in the water. The spear is not thrown. As the fish swims past the spear is driven through it and hoisted aloft at the same time; the same movement lands it on the bank off the point of the spear. When the water gets low enough brakes of bushes are pushed forward by several natives to shallow water, and the fish are then thrown on to the bank with the hands.

The natives have never learned to make either nets or fish-hooks.

Aranda welcoming dance. Entrance of the Strangers. Alice Springs, 1901.

4

COPING WITH A DRY COUNTRY, AND OTHER MATTERS

NOWHERE have I seen larger or more perfectly formed, or more diverse-shaped *pittjis* than the natives make in this same *wittjetti* country, of which Teatree Well may be regarded as a centre. From there it stretches for many miles in all directions. In dry seasons it is not well watered.

To reach and hunt for the grubs the lubras carry great *pittjis* full of water, with twigs of green leaves, or bunches of grass in them to keep the water from splashing as they walk. These are sometimes carried on the head, with a quoit-shaped ring made of twisted-up grass or string for a pad, the load being so heavy that another lubra lifts it upon the head of the bearer. Or it may be carried on the hip with a strong belt of string over the opposite shoulder and round the water-vessel, which is kept in horizontal position by the hand and arm. The art of carrying water in this way over rough stony country, and over plains densely covered with spinifex, is acquired by the young girls while in camp.

At the stations the women carry buckets full of water, or milk, on their heads without spilling a drop; if heavy they have to be lifted on and off by another person. Needless to say, by this method of carrying water the women acquire an upright gait and a stately, graceful habit in walking, that is much to be admired. I have often seen little girls at the stations carrying jam tins full of water on their heads. North of Alice Springs the *pittji* is more generally carried on the hip; but the art of carrying things on the head is ubiquitous. Some water *pittjis* I estimate would hold five gallons, and a lubra will carry one of these ten or twelve miles in a day without being greatly distressed.

The men also are of upright bearing, but they do not carry water; that is the women's portion. When they kill a kangaroo, wallaby, or emu, they disembowel it, roast and eat the entrails on the spot, and tie the four legs and head of the quarry tightly together so that the carcass makes a firm package, then a grass quoit for protection, similar to that the lubras make, is twisted, and the animal is carried to the camp on the head. It is really wonderful how they can carry a large kangaroo for miles over ranges and rough rocky ground. If night closes in they camp, and renew the march next day. The natives' joints are supple, and they appear to move along without effort. This is no doubt largely due to the amount of walking they have to do to gain the wherewithal to live.

The recognized rule among the natives is that the men hunt for game, and the women for seeds, yams, fruits, and bulbs. Neither, however, passes anything edible.

The craving for tobacco, in both sexes, is intense.

When they, for shame, refrain from begging for food or clothes, they will not hesitate to ask for tobacco. If you desire some article they possess and value, you can offer nothing more tempting than tobacco in exchange for it. More *tjurunga*, pointing bones, and weapons have been purchased from them by tobacco than by anything else. Only in recent years have the natives begun to value money as a medium of exchange for clothes, flour, tea, and sugar. Among themselves, or with a neighbouring tribe, bargaining for an article in exchange for another is an age-old practice. It is astonishing what great distances bartered articles travel in the course of years. That is why one sometimes sees articles in the natives' camps totally different in design from those made locally.

"Passing round the chewing-plug" of native tobacco is a curious and friendly custom among the natives. Having done the round and each person having had a chew, the owner places the quid over his ear, that being the best, safest, and most convenient place in which to carry it. *Ingulba* or *inkulba* is the native name for the plant; it is known as pituri by the whites. The substance is composed of the leaves, stems, and roots of a species of *Nieotiana*.[3] These are dried and ground up. In that form it is carried about, and sometimes used as a medium for barter with natives that live in localities where it does not grow.

I have watched them make a chewing-quid very often. They take from their ground-up supply a sufficient quantity, moisten it, and press it into the required shape. Then above it are burnt the twigs of a little bush so that the ashes fall upon the moistened quid, which is also rolled in the surplus ashes, and they are pressed into it. If a green or half-dry leaf of *ingulba* is available the quid is wrapped in it; if not, it is chewed without it. They say the ashes give the quid a better flavour, and a more potent grip.

Another way of making a chewing-quid - resorted to when the natives are at a spot where *ingulba* grows - is by partially drying the leaves in the sun, then steaming them in hot ashes, and beating the harder parts - stems and roots - with a stone to soften them; the mass is then worked to even consistency with the fingers and rolled into a plug, and ashes added as in the other case.

The drawing in of smoke to the mouth from a pipe they call drinking; hence, instead of saying "smoke a pipe," they say "drink a pipe."

While many of the foods are forbidden by the old men to women, and especially to pregnant women, as also to children and young men, I have never heard of a ban on tobacco to anyone. Strange to say, they use the same word, *mantera* or *mandera*, for clothes as for the little pouch - woven material made from threads of grass - in which they carry the *ingulba*.

Our tobacco is preferred to the native tobacco every time.

The Central Australian natives are fond of their dogs. But, if one may judge by their usual emaciated state, they must feed them largely on affection. They make no attempt to breed any particular kind of dog. Outback one often sees tamed dingoes in their camps, but mongrels, and plenty of them, are more often seen. Rarely does one see a dog that is fleet of foot enough to catch a full-grown kangaroo. They are, nevertheless, of great service to the natives in the way of discovering the whereabouts of rats, snakes, and lizards by scent, more especially in rocky ground, in thickets, or where the spinifex is dense. They save much time, and, as they run about a great deal, they find what might otherwise be missed.

At Winnecke's Depot, in the MacDonnell Ranges, I once saw in one of their camps what apparently was a kangaroo-dog of normal size, and so finely bred that it might have been taken for an Italian greyhound. Travellers who have done long stages in waterless country in hot weather with camels are familiar with the way the poor brutes dry up; their eyes stare from hollow sockets; their bellies shrivel up until one can nearly span around their loins, and all flesh sinks back and only skin stretches tightly from bone to bone. They can readily imagine what this dog was like. It was the nearest approach to a living skeleton I ever saw or imagined.

When my boy was asked what the natives did when they got as hungry as that, he replied that they buckled their belts up a bit tighter to avoid the empty feeling. When game is scarce the natives have to do quite a lot of buckling in, and for days together exercise the graces of patience and perseverance. When a native's appetite is satisfied, he is hilarious, and sings far into the night, and sometimes until-morning. When hungry he becomes a stoic.

Where formerly scores, even hundreds, of kangaroos were to be seen, one may now ride for a week and not see one. Kangaroo-rats were also plentiful, but they have nearly all disappeared; the "brakes," against which the natives used to drive them, have not been used for years, partly because white men have lent fire-arms to the natives. There are euros (scrub-kangaroos) and wallabies in the ranges, and from these the natives draw their largest supply of meat, of which they are passionately fond. These fall an easy prey to the native with a rifle.

When a beast is killed at a station it is customary to give the blacks the head, feet, lungs, and entrails, and often the heart and liver. They first empty, then clean the entrails by rubbing them in the sand. Every scrap of meat is eaten. It is an interesting sight to watch the bush natives, on the word being given, rush for the entrails like a pack of wolves, and drag them away. (The working boys get their portion separately; they are well and sufficiently fed by the stations.)

The natives do not cook the entrails thoroughly; just warm or grill them a little on the embers, then eat them with great relish, tearing at them like animals in a zoo. They never cook their meat thoroughly, saying it spoils to cook it much. And they tear away at meat on a bone just like an animal; when satisfied they throw it, as already stated, over the shoulder to the wife and children without saying a word. These do not portion it out. Each eats as much as she considers her share. then passes the bone to the next one entitled to a bit. It speaks volumes for their self-restraint that they only eat their proper portion; they never fail in this, however hungry they may be.

A peculiar deformity is sometimes seen in Central Australian natives - in young and old alike, and of both sexes. It is a forward bowing of the shin-bones, with, in some cases, a slight outward bowing as well. The space between the bones is considerably wider than normal. The legs of the natives thus affected are referred to by the whites as "boomerang legs." They certainly look very ugly; but in every case that came under my notice the individual appeared to be as strong, and as able to walk, as one not so afflicted. The cause has sometimes been ascribed to the prevailing custom, in some parts, of carrying very young children about in a deep wooden tray too short for the child to be able to extend itself properly.

In an article in the *Geographical Journal*, August 1935, on the results of an expedition to Lake Rudolf, East Africa, V. E. Fuchs, the leader, referred to a similar deformity in the Elmolo, a dwindling tribe that lives on the western shore of the lake, and who now number only eighty-four. The name Elmolo, Mr Fuchs says, means "poor or destitute ones." In 1887 the Elmolo lived on islands in the lake, but the retreating water of the lake has joined all of the islands to the mainland excepting one, on which there are two villages.

These people, he says, suffer from an almost universal deformity, a forward and sometimes outward bowing of the shin-bones, which may reach such a degree that it makes walking difficult, and gives the legs the appearance of having a second knee somewhere above the ankle. It seems certain, he adds, that the deformity is due to a diet deficiency. The Elmolo live entirely on fish, crocodiles, and turtles that are caught in the lake; and the only water they drink is that of the lake. It is known that there is little or no calcium in the lake waters, as it is precipitated by the soda-rich waters. Mr Fuchs's companion, Dr W. S. Dyson, found that the health of the Elmolo was bad, with a tendency to scurvy, pyorrhoea, decay of teeth, and arthritis. Another peculiarity was noticed: in eighty per cent of them the little toe was set far back on the foot.

Whether deficiency of lime, to which Mr Fuchs ascribes the bowed legs of the Elmolo, is the cause of the boomerang legs in the Central Australian natives, is not clear. The water the latter drink is ordinary ground water, from rock-holes, sand-soaks, or open waterholes, water that has drained off land, some of which is composed of limestone beds. Probably the deformity is due to some deficiency in the food, or in the food-supply, which in drought times is far too little, and that little the roughest and toughest; so much so that one wonders how the growing children manage to live at all on such poor stuff.

Sir William Mitchell informs me that Dr Cecil Hacket, of the University of Adelaide, has made an intensive investigation of boomerang leg and comes to another conclusion. In due course, I understand, Dr Hacket will make his conclusions public.

Hunting game is a fine art with the Central Australian native; which is not to be wondered at, seeing that their existence largely depends on the animals, birds, and reptiles they can catch. The art is interwoven; as already stated, with a wonderful knowledge of the habits of every living thing, by which deductions may be drawn from the smallest impressions - the tracks of a lizard in the sand, or of a snake.

On one of my return trips to Barrow from Victoria River, my only companions were two native boys and their lubras. We camped for the night on the sandy bed of Winnecke Creek, at a soakage called Ross Gap. As is their custom, the natives made a close inspection of the immediate surroundings; in doing so they came upon the trail of a snake on the bank, and ran it to a hollow log, half buried in the sand, quite close to where my blankets were spread. After assuring themselves that no trail led away from the log they said, "You must not camp there; a big snake is in that log." We set fire to one end of it and I, stick in hand, watched the other; sure enough out came, in due course, a seven-foot-long poisonous fellow. In summer the sun so heats the ground in the daytime that even snakes acquire nocturnal habits; for that reason the natives always make sure that no tracks are near where they sleep.

Once I pitched camp at a place called Boggy Waterhole, too late for the boys to see the tracks. The Finke River there makes sharp bends, and is hugged closely on both sides by high, rough, and for the most part impassable ranges, that cause any sound to re-echo. The mosquitoes being voracious, I was sleeping in my mosquito-net. It was bright moonlight. I was awakened sometime in the night by the natives shouting, dogs barking, and the ranges reverberating - a veritable pandemonium. I hurried to get out of my net, but the boys shouted:

"Get back in your net! There's a snake among the camel saddles, and he's quite close to you!"

I tucked the net under the blankets and had no sooner done so than the boys shouted:

"Don't move, he's by the side of your net."

The dog shifted it out of that and one of the boys threw a boomerang and killed it.

The natives are dead shots with either boomerang or spear if they can take aim. On the first outward journey I made to Victoria River I saw a very fine shot made by one of the bush natives with a spear. Far out from Barrow Creek we came across a dozen or more bush natives that showed themselves friendly. They offered to show us some of their waters in the spinifex sandhill country in the direction we wished to go.

Rats varying in size from that of a ferret to a rabbit are plentiful in the thick spinifex, as are our domestic cats gone wild, and the native spotted cat. The domestic ones have spread all over the interior; they grow to a large size there, and the natives kill and eat them. So plentiful were they at that time that my companions (I had three white men with me) often referred to it in later days as the Rat and Cat Country.

As the string of twenty camels strode along in single file the natives spread themselves out in half-moon shape and walked along in front of the string. When the rats raced from their lairs under the bunches of spinifex the natives threw boomerangs one after the other and rarely did a rat escape being killed. As they were killed the heads of the rats were tucked under the hair-string girdles of the natives, by night they had bagged enough cats and rats for a sumptuous feed. One rat became confused and crouched half under a tuft of spinifex. A native took good aim and drove his spear through it. It was a long shot and, had I not witnessed it, I would have thought it impossible, for the rat was no bigger than a kitten.

Travelling through localities thickly bushed, one occasionally sees a line of sticks and dry twigs. These represent former bush fences erected to guide rats or wallabies past some cover, behind which the natives hide until the animal approaches near enough to be boomeranged or speared. They are called "brakes" by the whites.

Those that I saw had not been repaired for many years, probably because of the scarcity of game.

The kangaroo-rat (commonly called "wide-awake") that runs with one arm straight out in front was formerly much more plentiful than today in the MacDonnell Ranges, and was frequently caught by means of brakes. It is good food even for whites.

Emus are very wild in those parts, and we were interested in the way the natives get them. Beyond Berry's Pass, in the western part of the above ranges, the waters are precarious. Two or three rain-water pools were fast drying up on one of the writer's visits to that part; they were all that remained on the Warren Creek, except waters in the sand. The emu must have water, so the natives had made camouflaged shelters of boughs on the banks overlooking these pools exactly resembling brushwood and flotsam brought down and piled against trees in flood-time, One was such a close imitation that we had to look twice to be convinced that it was artificial. These brakes were ten to fifteen feet long, and from two feet six inches to three feet high. Behind them the native waits patiently for hours at a stretch for his quarry, and while the emu drinks he receives his death-wound from a spear. When the pools are nearly dry, twigs of a poison bush (*Duboisia Hopwoodi*) are put in the water; this stupefies the emus which are then more easily caught, either with or without the help of their dogs.

When the locality to be hunted over lies at some distance from water (the natives know every rock-hole or sand-water within their beat) all the *pittjis* are filled, and a general exodus of men, women, children, and dogs takes place. I have witnessed many departures; some from large camps. The men usually lead off. They take a slow and very big drink before they start, and only carry their spears, spear-throwers, boomerangs, and a fire-stick. The fire-sticks are replenished from time to time, and are used to fire the spinifex and thickets for any game that may be sheltering there. They soon separate, to cover as wide a strip of ground as possible.

The women, with much shouting from camp to camp and calling for dogs, follow, laden with water, yam-sticks, nulla-nullas, *pittjis* (in which are hair-and bark-string, bound-up *tjurunga*, stone knives, ochre, personal adornments such as necklaces of string or beans, headbands, kangaroo teeth set in spinifex gum or what not) children and dogs that cannot or will not follow. Originally there were no clothes or blankets to carry; all were naked. But of late years some possess both, and the blankets are carried by the women. They also gather seeds, fruits, bulbs, yams, grubs, lizards, and snakes while on the journey. The contents of their *pittjis* after a day's hunt are surprising in their variety; often very rough stuff, but filling if not very nourishing.

If the way be long, the children young, and the weather hot, the father will often carry his children in turn. He does this by placing the child on his neck with legs banging in front, and for support the child clings to his head. I have seen a woman carrying one child that way, another on one hip with her arm around it, and a *pittji* on the other hip with her arm over it and a yam-stick in that hand. Sometimes she carries one child, a dog, and a *pittji*. One or more of the women in each party invariably carry fire-sticks.

They are never in doubt as to the whereabouts of any member of the party or the direction in which he or she may have gone; for they know the footprints of every one, and can if necessary follow them. They frequently signal to one another by means of smokes. In this way they cover long distances, make dry camps between the waters, and gather their food as they go.

As regards conveying messages by means of smoke-signals, the late. A. T. Magarey collected, or tried to collect information through many years, but apparently without much success. This is what Strehlow was able to gather from the natives at the Finke Mission Station:

When a man is approaching a friendly camp of natives he intimates to them his presence by making a great smoke, by setting fire to coarse grass, or failing grass, dry bushes. Should a member of, say, a hunting expedition become separated from the other members, perhaps outdistanced by them, or they by him, and they espy him taking a little rest, he signals to his friends by making two smokes rise close to one another.

In the event of him unexpectedly coming upon a large camp of natives he apprises them by making four smokes rise side by side. Neither the Aranda nor the Loritja people know any other smoke-signals than these.

I have watched the natives making fire often enough; in fact, have made it myself in the same way. The native, if possible, finds a dry stick with a crack-opening in it; or, failing that, splits one and props it open with a small stick. He fills the crack with dry soft grass, or bark, rubbed to tinder. Over the tinder, across the crack, he places the thin edge of his hardwood spear-thrower, and pressing down hard rubs to and fro. If another man be present he sits opposite, holding the other end of the spear-thrower, both men pressing and rubbing together. Sparks soon fly into the tinder, and by gentle blowing burst into flame. In three or four minutes the fire is made. The writer has purchased several shields with a short deep furrow cut into them, across which furrow were the marks of the spear-thrower contact.

The so-called spinifex gum is a resin that exudes from the stems of a species of spinifex Troidea that grows on or around the base of rocky ranges. The globules are the size of radish-seed and, like gum, they dry hard. The women root out the stems with a yam-stick, and with it beat them on a flat bare rock if such be near, or failing that, on a hard bare patch of ground. The stems are thrown away and the chaff and most of the dirt are winnowed from the gum. The residue is melted by holding a fire-stick above it and pressing it into a lump. This is then worked up on a stone by ironing it out, doubling it, and so forth, with another hot stone, until a pitch-like substance results that will set like a rock. This is the substance with which they fix handles on stone axes and stone knives, set cutting-stones in adzes, fasten spears. and use for many other purposes: for example, plugging holes in their water-troughs. As it can be softened by heat it can be pressed into any shape. The natives carry a reserve stock about with them.

Arrernte child asleep in a *pittji*. Alice Springs 1895.

5

HEREDITARY TRAITS AND OTHER THINGS

THE aborigines are great walkers. For that reason they are often employed by station owners and others to take written messages to neighbouring stations, which may be fifty miles away. Bush natives are mostly chosen to take the letters. They call them "paper yabber" (paper talk).

The usual procedure is to wrap the envelope in thick paper, split a twig, insert the package in the split, and tie the split end, so that the native carries it by a handle. The letter then takes the place of a passport; armed with it he requires no other weapon to ensure his safe passage through unfriendly tribes. He is given at starting enough food to see him through the journey, and the receiver gives him another letter and food for the return journey. It is really wonderful the pace at which the real wild native travels to convey a paper yabber.

Among themselves messengers are often sent with verbal messages to distant tribes. In this case they are given a message-stick - a small stick with burnt-in markings thereon-and that stick is his passport.

The following will give some idea of their capacity to travel quickly: We were driving with a four-in-hand from Teatree Well to the Hanson Well on the Overland Telegraph Line one scorching hot day, and arrived at the latter place between two and three in the afternoon. A native followed shortly after we left. When we were un-harnessing the horses, to our surprise the native turned up, apparently little the worse for his thirty-mile walk. I have known boys of eleven and twelve years, with the help of a drink or two of water, walk thirty miles in a day.

They do not mind walking a long way in search of horses or camels that have strayed overnight; but even the wild ones object to walking back, preferring to ride, or try to ride, almost any animals that will let them get on their backs. This was brought home to me in rather a painful way (for the native) while camped at Burt Well on one occasion. Burt Well is thirty-five miles north of Alice Springs, on the telegraph line. A wild native had accompanied one of my working boys to hunt up the horses one morning. Later, the horses came galloping to the troughs, and one had only a bridle on.

Soon afterwards three or four boys hove in sight, and one of them, I saw, was injured. The others hastened to explain that the injured native "would get on," and as often as he did the mare threw him off; not that she was vicious, but the boy was green from the bush and could not ride. He had at length fallen on his wrist and badly dislocated it. We attended to the injury there and then, and in a couple of months he was trying to ride again.

They are ambitious to learn to ride, and do not mind a few falls in acquiring the art.

Most of the boys[4] handle horses gently, and, as the natives have untold patience with them, the animals gain confidence, and will let them catch and handle them without fear. So these boys make very useful stockmen under proper supervision.

They handle camels equally well. For several years I was engaged in transporting provisions and general merchandise from the railhead to all parts of the interior, and used black boys exclusively. The string consisted always of not less than forty camels, more often fifty, on one occasion as many as eighty on a journey of over five hundred miles. Each camel had its load, and they averaged five camels to the ton. The boys hunted up the camels each morning; saddled and loaded them; kept the loads evenly balanced while on the march, and unsaddled and hobbled them out in the evening.

I cooked their food; cut and gave each boy his portion separately and kept the saddles in good order. Starting on the journey the boys were supplied with a complete suit of clothes, hat, boots, belts, and knives; and as things wore out they were given others from a reserve stock that was carried. All were supplied with blankets. At the end of each journey they received a little money, which they straightway squandered, or gambled away.

It will thus be seen that, under proper, kindly supervision the Australian natives are capable of very useful work. They come to work as raw savages, naked and unable to speak or understand a word of English. Under kindly, sympathetic, just treatment, they quickly undergo a wonderful transformation - but only along lines that coincide with their natural gifts. In other directions their mentality is very low; some never learn how to tie a knot a rope correctly; others learn quickly. Much patience is necessary in handling them at first.

But when they become familiar with the work, they repay it all. They learn pidgin-English, and are able to speak it in a short while, infinitely more quickly than the whites learn any native language. When my boys were taken among tribes with a different language they used English as the medium to communicate with them. Their sense of locality is simply wonderful, uncanny. Their powers of observation and knowledge of bushcraft are superb. Pioneers who have had the wit to see and utilize those gifts have found them most useful helpers. No small portion of the credit for finding natural waters, and opening up the dry interior, should rightly be ascribed to the natives.

To make useful helpers the natives, of both sexes, require to be taken in hand young, the younger the better; then they more readily assimilate the white man's or white woman's ideas and ways of doing things. I once heard an old bushman expatiate on the impossibility of teaching the matured natives to do even the simplest of jobs. His peroration ran:

"You can take it from me, for real out and out stupidity you can't beat a blackfellow."

The aspersion was true enough from his standpoint, no doubt; but had the situation been reversed and he, say, had been given a spear and boomerang and told to forage for himself in that wilderness, would he have shaped any better. It is all a matter of traditional education. The natives' intellectual status being away back in the Stone Age, they cannot comprehend and execute things of which they have no knowledge or experience. They can learn to do things well enough in directions where their mentality bas been exercised through many generations; but their backward state, mentally, in directions that have never been required to maintain their existence appears at every turn. That is the real reason for their lack of comprehension - or as the old bushman described it, "real out and out stupidity."

The training of boys to be useful is not always easy while they are living among their own people. On the roads, or a way from parental influences, they are more tractable. The confidence with which parents will hand over their children to whites whom they know, is surprising, even though the child may not be returned to them for months.

The daily round of a camel boy's life runs something like this: At daylight he hears that hateful word, *akaraeri* (wake up). He then begins to stretch and yawn. Fain would he have slept for another hour. It is a hard struggle, but eventually he sits up, slips on his boots, picks up a nose-line and hurries off with a shambling gait in the direction the camels went the night before. He may be accompanied by one or more of the other boys, and the plan of hunt has probably been discussed and agreed upon the night before. In any case some of the boys keep outside all tracks on one side, and the rest do the same on the other, so that if the spread of the mob be normal they will outflank every camel, the hunters from both sides will meet, and drive the whole mob to camp.

Having caught them, each camel is led to and set down between his own load. The boys then work in pairs, for some of the saddles are heavy; two of them grip the saddle-sticks and throw the saddles, one after the other, on to the camels' backs as quickly as possible. That done each boy attends to his own ten camels and fixes the cruppers and breast-plates. No girths are used.

He then gets his own wad of food, his billycan of tea, and his pannikin, takes them to the best. shade he can see, sits down with all the other boys, eats a hearty breakfast and enjoys a good rest. Boys that have their lubras eat with them separately. Lubras are fed just like the boys. They collect firewood, light the fire, boil the meat - great pieces of salt beef in a five-gallon drum, and sometimes cook the dampers for the boys' food.

While the boys are eating their breakfast we will note sundry things about the camel.

We all have our little fancies and dislikes. Most Europeans seem to regard the camel as little more than an ungainly, strong-smelling brute. Station people especially have next to no time for him because he frightens the horses. Why this is so is not known, for they get scared and tremble and bolt even if they do not smell him.

The natives say that the shape of the front half of a camel bears some resemblance to an emu, and the movement of his head and neck as he walks, they say, is "just like an emu." The late W. A. Horn, of the Horn Scientific Exploring Expedition, once described a camel as "a composite sort of thing, the front half of him being an emu, and the hind half a kangaroo, with a bad splice between. "

Very few Europeans really take to camels; fewer still acquire the art of working them successfully. As with most of the useful callings in life, one bas to serve a lengthy, severe apprenticeship at the game before one can transport heavy loads over long distances with them without giving them sore backs. Never yet have I found a native with sufficient intelligence to be able to do that, they can be of great assistance all the same. In the early days a camel was a never-ending source of wonder to the native. The way he lies down, the way he gets up, the tremendous load he is able to get up with, and carry all day, and day after day without a drink, were things he could not comprehend.

A horse, as everyone knows, lies with his legs to one side, and gets up by raising his forequarters first; then his hind quarters with a sudden spring forward. With such action no animal can rise with a heavy load on its back. A camel, on the other hand, lies straight on his stomach, just like a cat. He rests on his brisket and the joints above his knees in front and above the hocks behind. These five bearing surfaces, all calloused, make a solid foundation, and the arched back completes an ideal weight-carrying structure. All four feet are tucked snugly under him.

The saddles being on and breakfast eaten, the boys now start to lift on forty or fifty great loads. This is the hardest work they have to do, and they know it, so off come their coats, and their shirts too if the day be hot. Two boys lift half the load on one side of the camel, and two the other half on the other side; the head boy then ties the ropes, a swag or other top-load is placed between the packages, which a top-rope holds in place.

A boy on each side now steadies the great load (between five and seven hundredweight) as the animal stiffens his muscles to rise with it. A gentle touch with the toe of the boot on the side and the camel gently straightens his hind legs, which action hoists his hind quarters up, and he then spreads his hind legs wide apart. His knees and two hind legs now form a tripod. In that position he gets one knee and foreleg free, doubles the foot of it backwards and places the lower end of the shank-bone on the ground. This front leg and the two hind legs form a second tripod, and that enables him to get the other front leg free. With three legs free he forms a third tripod and that enables him to straighten the other front leg. and the camel is on his feet. The movements of course follow in quick succession and the casual observer may not notice them; but without resorting to such tactics a camel, strong as he is, could not rise with that weight on his back. Once on his feet he can carry the load all day.

A boy then leads him away, ties him to the crupper of the camel in front, and returns to help load the next camel. No time is lost; the boys work with a will to get the job over. In doing so they sweat like horses, and the aroma they exhale is always pungent, sometimes quite overpowering.

As the loading of the whole string takes an hour or two, to prevent those loaded from pushing against one another, a thing they are much given to do, a lubra or spare boy leads them very slowly round and round the camp.

When the last load (two large tucker-boxes) is on, the word *kulla* (finished) is heard and the string moves off and never stops until the appointed stage is done - unless something goes wrong. Hour after hour you hear the groan of the swaying loads, and the gentle pit pat of the camels' feet as they place them in correct position on the ground. The heavy loads they carry might over-balance them if hurried out of their stride.

Camels should always be allowed to travel at their own gait, which averages about two and a half miles an hour.

Each boy is supposed to know his ten camels, and be able to place each between its own load, and by its own saddle. He rides on one of his loaded camels. When one of the ten breaks a nose-line, or a load is leaning to one side he is supposed to attend to it. For broken nose-lines a halt is rarely made; but to straighten a load it is occasionally necessary.

If any of the boys has a sensible lubra his ten camels are placed first in the string and she rides on the leading camel; keeps him on the pad, and makes the pace such that the whole loaded string can keep up with ease. If she makes the pace too fast, snap goes a nose-line; if too slow, the camels push against each other and disarrange the loads. In either case her name is anathema, for the injury done takes valuable time to set right.

For a few minutes after starting the boys walk by the string to push up any load that is leaning to one side. As soon as everything is going satisfactorily, each reckons. he might as well ride. On one of the camels his swag is placed between the load for a seat.

He has already learned how to mount a camel while it is walking along. This he does in the following way. He gets in close to the neck of the camel, and while walking there puts both hands on the neck, then making a leap lands with his stomach on the neck, and his body in horizontal position. By struggling he gets his left shin on the neck; uprights himself by grasping the saddle-sticks; gets one foot on the neck of the camel, and climbs from there to his seat on the top of the load. If a nose-line breaks, or a load goes awry, he slides down the way he got up; does the mending, and up again in quick time without halting the march.

This acrobatic feat of jumping off and on while the string is in motion requires time and practice to acquire; the antics of new boys learning it afford lookers-on no end of merriment, especially the boys who have mastered the art. Boys that are tall enough to grip the sticks of the saddle sometimes make a step and a spring and land on the camel's neck with the left knee over, and from there climb to the top of the load. The animals they ride are quiet of course.

It is a singular thing that both horses and camels will allow black boys they know to handle them without flinching, often to crawl all over them, while at the same time they may be very suspicious of a white man. Travelling from Alice Springs to Deep Well on one occasion I had this fact brought home to me in a very painful way.

I had been making some improvements to the above well and some business matters required a trip to Alice Springs, fifty miles distant. Having completed what I bad to do there, I was offered a ride back to Deep Well with an empty caravan of camels, on its way to Oodnadatta. The caravan was owned and driven by an Afghan I knew well. When camped abreast of Ooraminna Rockhole it was found necessary to change my mount for some reason or other, and I was given a camel that one of the boys had been riding for months past, and that would allow him to climb on and off in the way just described. "Era nama roka" (she is quiet), the boy said, as I proceeded to arrange my blankets on the pack-saddle to make a comfortable seat. I had refused the Afghan's kind offer to lend me his riding-saddle. It did not occur to me that the animal would take offence at a stranger.

All was ready to start, I got on, and the whole string was stood up. I noticed my mount looking at me as she moved her head from side to side, then she gave a couple of very strong bucks and the saddle with me on it was fired heavenwards as from a catapult. I landed first and the saddle came down on top of me. When consciousness returned, one leg and hip were quite numb and I suspected very serious injuries. The boy who had been riding the camel was in great distress, seeming to take the blame upon himself.

Fortunately no bones were broken, but I carried great bruises, and was a lame duck for months, all through trying to ride a camel that was tame for a blackfellow. When recovered sufficiently to travel I was given another and more reliable mount, and in due course we arrived at Deep Well. There another incident occurred to a small black boy.

Deep Well at the time I am writing about was leased by the contractor who carried the mail on camels between Oodnadatta and Alice Springs, making the round trip, if I remember rightly, every fortnight. The string on this particular trip consisted of six camels. A little boy was the only assistant the mailman had with him. While he and the boy had their lunch the camels were left standing. For some reason they became restless, and refused to stand still. The boy was told to hobble them. As he proceeded to do so they started pushing one another and ringing around. One of them knocked the boy over and another trod on his leg midway between the knee and ankle. We rushed to his assistance, pulled him out from under them, and found that both bones were broken.

The leg was set and put in splints; a wurley was built over him where he lay, and with good nourishing food the boy was soon able to walk about on crutches. When he found the leg growing stronger he assured me that the bone had never been broken, "only bent."

A characteristic of the Central Australian natives is lack of thoroughness. What they are set to do they will shirk in part if that be the easier course. They cannot be relied on to carry out instructions to the letter. They will, as already stated, only half water animals in the heat of summer if they feel tired, or lazy. They will see a load hanging out of plumb for hours while on the march and not set it upright, knowing all the time that it is causing a sore on the animal's back. This lack of thoroughness in what they do means much unnecessary work for them at times.

Now, there are no worse ramblers than camels; sometimes they give the boys very long walks to overtake them. You can tell the boys as often as you like to bobble them short; but, unless you see that it is done, they will persist in giving them the full length of the chain, although they know that it will mean a great walk in the morning.

A case in point occurred between Crown Point and Horseshoe Bend on one of my trips. It was the middle of summer and the heat was terrific. We had camped on a patch of green feed near the Finke crossing the previous night, and the camels had been "in clover." When we camped near Horseshoe Bend I warned the boys:

"Be sure and short hobble the camels or they will make back to the green feed."

Having other things to attend to, I did not see to it that every camel was short hobbled. Away went the boys after them in the morning. Those that had been short hobbled scattered widely but were brought back about midday by all the boys save one. The boy that was away was trustworthy and stuck to the tracks of the missing seven camels. As none of them were riding-camels he would have to walk and drive them all the way back. The heat was so intense that I feared the boy would perish of thirst. His mates were greatly concerned also, and kept a sharp look out from an eminence close by.

About four o'clock some camels were seen in the distance coming very slowly along the road from our last camp. As they drew nearer the boys all strained their eyes to see if the boy was there. At last they saw him a long way behind the camels; they said he was staggering. One of them rushed for a water-bag and off along the road as fast as he could go. The others saw the boy fall and cried:

"He's done! He's done!"

And away they went too. They carried him into camp. His tongue was so swollen it was difficult for him to swallow or speak. Eventually we got him round and by questioning discovered that he found the camels at the former green camp, fifteen miles away, and that they were all long hobbled.

Serious as this lesson was they still chose the easier road of hobbling the camels full length unless they were watched.

The work the boys have to do when attached to a string of pack-camels is not without a certain amount of risk from bites as well as kicks. The risk is not wholly confined to a boy's own string. So it is small wonder that, when opportunity offers, they even things up a bit. The danger time for bites is when the bull camels come on in season. Animals that are docility itself, and may be led and handled by a child, then undergo a complete change in disposition and habits. They even have a disregard - I had almost said contempt - for their food then; they wander about lashing their tails, blowing their bladders, and holding their heads high in challenge to other bulls. Some of them are very skilful fighters.

I once owned a small red Mekranie bull that was a champion; he feared no camel, even if twice his size. Muscular and thick-set, he had tusks, top and bottom, quite as large as any lion or tiger; in fact, the resemblance was very striking. All mature bulls have similar tusks.

The camel's knock-out blow, so to say, is to get his opponent down. There are two ways of doing it: in the usual, but less effective way, one gets his neck over the neck of his opponent and presses it low enough to enable him to grip the front leg above the knee, when the animal is forced to lie down; then by degrees the top bull slides along, gets his brisket on his opponent's head and flattens it.

In the other way - and it was the one my bull always adopted - the bull gets shoulder to shoulder, and spars about and bites the feet and legs of his opponent until he can reach the off hind leg, low down. Having secured a firm grip he draws the leg to him and with a push of his shoulder the unfortunate animal falls on his side. Once down he has small chance of getting up again, and the end comes in precisely the same way.

How many bulls mine killed I cannot say, but we knew of several. While he lasted, my string was fairly safe from any stray bulls along the road. The boys were sorry when he died.

One of these marauding brutes was a lame bull whose beat lay between Charlotte Waters and Horseshoe Bend. He would link on to any travelling caravan and follow it, miles behind in the daytime, and get among the string in the night. Being a good fighter, not-withstanding his lameness, he gave the boys and me a lot of anxiety. I was much relieved to hear from my boys that the boys belonging to a caravan ahead of mine had got rid of him. Now, you cannot deceive a native in his own line. So when my boys told me how the boys in the other caravan had got rid of him I knew it was a fact, although I felt incredulous until I saw how they had done it.

We were camped for the night a little to the north of the Crown Point Finke crossing. While the boys were out for the camels in the morning they discovered their old enemy, the marauding bull, dead and on his back in a very narrow gulch opening out of the hills that border the road there.

I asked how the boys' got him in. "They pushed him in, " I was told. My boys described how the others had caught him; blindfolded him by tying an old shirt over his eyes; led him carefully close to the bank, and with a united push sent him over. As my caravan passed near the spot an hour or two later, I went over and found that the boys had described the incident quite accurately. I was glad for the road to be rid of such a pest.

I nearly lost my life on one occasion, and owe it to my boys for the instantaneous and fearless way they attacked the camel that had hold of me. The incident happened one morning when we were saddling up the camels at a camp between Attack Creek and Banka-Banka station. The boys were busy at their saddles, and I was leaning against the flank of my riding-camel trying to reach the girth that lay under him, when I noticed his breathing, and felt his soft lips on my ear. He was an exceptionally quiet animal, and always treated by the boys and myself as a pet.

Now, nature has provided a camel with very powerful jaws, and molar teeth that will grind up the hardest and toughest of twigs and leaves. In addition to that he is able to stretch his jaws exceptionally wide, far wider than a horse. As his food is largely gathered from prickly bushes such as prickly Acacias, he has to open his mouth wide. With his long, sensitive, delicately soft lips he works all the thorns forward, closes his mouth on them gently and then pulls them off the twig by stripping it; a bite or two on it then and down the mouthful goes, there to stay until he finds time to chew his cud.

When my camel's soft lips came against my ears I paid little attention. I had felt them against my face many times before. It was not until I felt his jaws closing over my shoulder and chest that I realized what was happening, my face being turned away from him as I reached for the girth. He had me firmly in his grip; it was like a vice. As he closed his jaws, which he did gradually, I felt my chest sinking in. I screamed, and the boys ran with sticks and made him let go, when I fell over helpless, but not unconscious.

The boys undid my shirt to see what harm the tusks had done. The animal, fortunately for me, was young and his tusks only half grown, but one had injured one of my ribs. I still have a lump there. For several days I had great difficulty and pain in breathing. When I was able to reach Banka, my old and lamented friend, the late Arthur Ambrose, showed me great kindness until I could travel.

Meanwhile the boys had kept the camels and loading intact, and shown in their own way much concern for my welfare.

6

TRAINING YOUNG FIGHTERS

THE elderly men no doubt give the boys advice in the art of throwing the spear and boomerang, but I have never seen them instruct a group of boys. Probably the boys are supposed to acquire the art by practice. This they do from the time they can hold a reed in their hand. As soon as they are able to run strongly they practise the art of self-defence. Dodging and diverting the spear and boomerang with a shield are the two methods of defence, and the boys get skilful at it. To imitate the boomerang they use flat chips of wood, short bits of bark, or at the stations bits of board, or anything that will turn end on end when thrown.

A favourite missile is a thick piece of bark, of the size and shape of a lengthwise section through a football. They play games with these. Sides are taken, and each combatant holds as many pieces of bark as he can, with a spare stock on the ground as well. At the signal arranged they commence throwing at one another as fast as they can with the object of driving the opposing force back. On each side, some are deputed to pick up the missiles thrown by the opposing party. Once I watched a great game in which about thirty young men and boys took part. The battle waged hot and strong, and the excitement equalled that of a game of football. Again and again one side would drive the other right off the ground; later, the reverse would happen. This went on the whole afternoon.

The children and young people are fond of games.

Boys' games are more boisterous than those of girls and young women. The girls are naturally gentle in habit, and most are shy and retiring. One rarely meets with a rollicking girl, partly because they are constantly checked by the old women. The boys, on the other hand, are full of fun, and their merry laugh is exhilarating. Only at the puberty stage is real restraint placed upon them; they are then made to camp with the unmarried men. The maidens camp together in charge of a chaperone.

Both children and adults are fond of personal decoration.

Young children are mostly carried on the hip, on which they sit astride, with the mother's arm around them. They are hoisted on with one hand only, by a firm grip on the child's arm close to the shoulder. The way the father carries a child has been already described. Children, even in infancy, have no protection in the way of clothes. They are weaned very late - two years or more; up to four years unless a second child is forthcoming when, like an animal, the elder has to give place to the younger. Children are given meat to eat when very young. As already stated, rubbing with sand, or earth, is the method adopted for washing a child. Young children are rarely checked, and are allowed to cry as much as they like; but as a rule they are very quiet, and seem able to entertain themselves.

Native boys do what I have never seen anyone else attempt - handle scorpions. Scorpions in that country appear to live in colonies; at any rate certain camps seemed to be infested with them. My memory recalls two camps at which one at least of our party was sure to see a scorpion, even if one was not found under someone's blankets in the morning. The natives know the shape of the hole a scorpion digs for himself in the sandy loam. If they want to make their camp on such a spot. they either dig the scorpions out or plug the holes up securely. Usually they select another spot.

One of these scorpion colonies was situated at a camp known as the "Second Tent Hill Water," on Tempe Downs station. Several boys, about twelve years old, were engaged to assist in shifting a mob of cattle to that water. From the station to the water is a day's ride on horseback. The pad leads along the Walker Creek. All the way one is hemmed in by flat-topped ranges, sometimes close at hand, but receding to five and six miles away. The last eight or ten miles, through the Walker Gorge, are extremely picturesque. The gorge is only wide enough for the meandering channel of the Walker Creek. From the sandy bed of the creek the dark red sandstone walls rise sheer four to six hundred feet on both sides. The only way through the ranges is by this gorge, and, because of its sinuous course, red walls terminate the view at short range all around. It is a more impressive spectacle even than the celebrated "Glen of Palma," in the Krichauff Ranges; the walls are equally high, and the gorge is narrower. I shall never forget the awe I experienced the first time I rode through it. It is one of the most remarkable physical features in Central Australia. Once through the gorge the tent-shaped hill that gives the water its name comes into view.

From my camp at the water I noticed that the boys were intent on digging out something, so I walked over and watched them. They at length reached the bottom of the hole they had followed by keeping a small green twig in the hole and always pushing it a little ahead of where they were digging. When the stick reached the end of the hole, with care and caution, they extracted a scorpion unhurt.

The next act was to handle it. This was done with the help of two small straight twigs. An end of one of the sticks was placed across the two claws, and the other end on the ground, and that stick was kept down by the fingers of one hand. With the other hand the other stick was similarly placed across the tail. Then the fingers of each hand were gently moved along the sticks, meanwhile keeping the scorpion pinned tightly until both tail and claws were secured by the fingers and thumb of each hand. Each hand worked separately and secured its own claws, or tail, as the case might be, and the boys took no risks. Once properly secured they carried the creatures about; to get rid of them they dashed them down very smartly.

As it is not definitely known what the "pubic tassel" signifies I will refer to it here. The pubic tassel, variously called warrabakana or *albata*, is a small tuft of rat-tail tips tied like a bouquet, or sometimes of many short lengths of string made of hair or fur, tied together in the middle with both ends loose. The string that binds in each case also affixes the tassel to the pubic hairs.

My own impression is that the natives regard it as exclusively a masculine adornment. The small size ($2^{1/2}$ inches in diameter) is proof that it was never intended for what the Germans call "a shame-covering." The natives originally wore no clothing or coverings of any sort, and apparently saw no need for covering the genital organs; nor do they still, except when in the company of whites. The women remove most of their pubic hairs; scarcely sufficient are left to which to attach a pubic tassel even if they wished to do so.

One of the most striking adornments worn by the men is the glistening white forehead-band, usually woven in one piece like a very broad tape, with strings to tie behind the head. Sometimes, instead of this, a long hair cord is wound round and round the head. This is generally coloured red, with red ochre and grease; the tape-band is whitened with chalk, or the white substance on the limewood-trees (*Eucalyptus papuana*), called *ilumba* by the natives.

Another masculine fashion that must be very awkward when sleeping, is to pull all the hair of the head tightly back and slightly upwards, and bind it round very many times with a cord. This cord is also made of wallaby or opossum hair, The men wear a similar cord armband (all in one piece) that fits firmly above the muscle on the arm. Then there is the man's cord girdle for the waist, made of human hair-usually from his mother-in-law's head; sometimes the hair, it is said, comes from his father-in-law's head.

One often sees the black and red tail-feathers of the black cockatoo, or the white feathers of the white cockatoo, stuck in the young men's hair.

The women wear a cord of wallaby hairs wound round and round the head, to which rat-tail tips are frequently fixed as end pendants; this much-prized decoration is called *kanta*. The cord is well greased and coloured with red ochre. The neckband is often in one piece, composed of about six

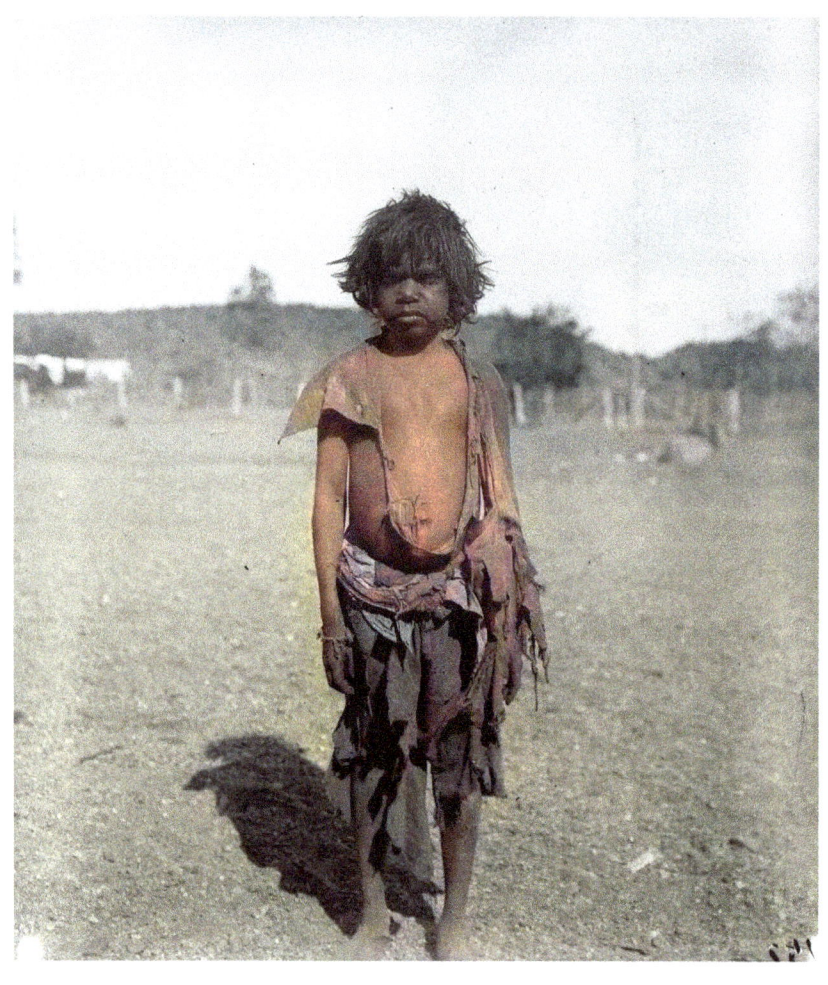

Aranda boy wearing cast-off clothing at Alice Springs station, 1901.

smaller. cords bound from side to side to form a ribbed ribbon, that can be tied at the back of the neck; or the neckband may be one long cord wound round and round the neck; this is called *wallabanba*. I have seen three or four, all with tassel ends, worn at the same time, and all shining with grease and red ochre. Strings of Stuart's bean-tree beans are made by boring a hole through the beans with a hot wire and putting a string through them. How they managed to bore (or burn) these holes before the whites brought wire I don't know. Probably prior to that they only mounted them, as they still do, in a setting of spinifex gum.

Some further reference to their personal decorations is made in the chapter "Cicatrices and Mutilations."

The following information regarding the colours used, and what they signify, is given by Strehlow: The colouring of the body, and of the implements and weapons, is reproduced from what their forefathers taught and practised. They adhere tenaciously to what is related in the traditions. The different colours often have a definite meaning. White is the universal colour for mourning and grief. If a man dies, his wife bedaubs herself all over (hair included) with a paste of white chalk, partly out of grief for the dead, and partly that the ghost of her lamented husband may not recognize her. An avenger draws a white streak along his nose to show the occupants of another camp that he will supplant them, and to. show that the bones of his victims will soon bleach: Black is the colour of a completed avenging tour. The returned blood-avenger, for example, marks himself with stripes of black, the number corresponding with the number of persons killed. Yellow is the colour of glowing fire, and means anger and lust for combat. Red is the colour for joy, the love-colour; it is the favourite colour of the natives. In festivities they not only cover themselves with red, but they besmear their wood and stone *tjurungas* with red ochre. In the marriage ceremony both bride and bridegroom are red ochred. The colouring of the widow red at the grave of her husband is a sign that her mourning-time is ended.

Of the rock-paintings Strehlow says: They are thought by the men, women, and children to have been made by the totem-forefathers when they travelled over the country, particularly the wild-cat forefathers. They placed the hands of men, feet of kangaroos, rock-wallabies or emus there. The men regard the rock-paintings only as decorations.

7

THE MAGICIAN AND SUPERSTITION

THE natives have some very strange customs. We camped at Henbury, a station on the Finke River, we found on one occasion a woman blind with ophthalmia, both eyes being swollen to a great size. A magician decided that some enemy had propelled bones from a distance into her eyes, which bones must be extracted. This he proceeded to do by sucking out the bones with his mouth. The screams of the poor patient acquainted us of the fact that something was wrong, so we went over to see what was the matter. By sleight-of-hand he showed us pebbles and bits of bone that he pretended he extracted from her eyes.

While doing some repairs to Burt Well one of my employees nearly recovered from some internal complaint. Being a bit of a wag he decided to call in one of these magicians. The magician's terms, half a stick of tobacco, were accepted, and the operation began. The man was laid on his side and the magician felt and pressed the seat of the complaint, much in the same way that a surgeon would do, then started sucking the spot with considerable vigour, making a bubbling noise with his mouth. Secreted in his mouth, he had a quantity of pebbles and bits of bone. With apparently Herculean efforts he would extract one and show it, then have another go, and another stone was shown, and so on until his supply had become exhausted. The rogue then declared the patient would recover, and received payment.

Sucking is not the only method of curing practised by magicians in Central Australia. On the Finke (this happened at Henbury too) a woman was troubled by severe stomach pains. She was taken to a tree with an overhanging branch and told to lie down underneath. The magician then grasped the overhanging limb and began treading the stomach of the woman into the right consistency, regulating the pressure by the help of the branch above.

Several years ago I was passing Macumba station, on the Macumba Creek, and saw a hideous sight - a boy with his lips cut off. On asking the reason I was told that when a child the boy would not stop crying. The magicians in council decided that the only cure for the malady was to cut the child's lips off.

The faith held in the magician's art by many of the natives. can sometimes prove fatal. If a magician tells his patient there is no hope for him, the patient makes up his mind to die; and die he does, not-withstanding that the case may be quite a curable one. Or a perfectly healthy individual may be told that a bone will be propelled into him by some enemy, which will cause him to sicken and die.

Here is a case in point: At Tennant's Creek Telegraph Station the old native who had chopped the firewood for years had been told that enemies had evil designs on him. For a long time he managed to thwart them by giving them no chance to get a shot at him. On one of my later visits to the station the manager met me, and among the first things he said was:

"They got him in the end."

"Got whom?" I asked. I had forgotten that my friend had told me that he would lose his woodchopper some day, having been warned that the old man was to be "boned." During my absence someone had been deputed to inform the old chap that while he was in a certain place his enemies had managed to get a shot at him from some cover, which was pointed out to him. He believed the tale, took ill, and was soon dead.

My boys, indeed all the natives I have known, seemed to have the greatest fear of death. At times they were filled with superstitious imaginings of all sorts; some great ill they thought was pending, or something was coming to harm them; they would relate that they had seen all sorts of scarecrows. These occasions would usually be on still evenings, the precursors of storms of wind or rain. They would then only speak in whispers, and always persuade a companion to accompany them if they had to leave the camp, both armed with boomerangs.

On one occasion a celebrated rain-maker had to enlist the help of other magicians and sundry old men to help him break the drought that for a long time past had held Deep Well in an iron grip.[5] To this end they performed many secret ceremonies. They then went to the ranges and, standing on the top of one, waved in circles eaglehawk's wings held in both hands, to draw in their direction the promising clouds that were rising. The rain came, and continued far too long for the rain-maker's comfort; so he again enlisted the help of his former assistants to stop it. This was accomplished by the whole of them shouting their loudest, and striking at the rain with sticks, and assuming all sorts of threatening attitudes. After this notable success he was regarded by all as a specialist at the game.

Instances of how firmly the natives believe in the current stories of terrifying monsters dwelling in well-known waters, frequently came under my notice. One of the best-known stories relates to the monster said to dwell in the large waterhole in the Finke Gorge. The story now to be related is of a snake that had his home in a natives' well out in the sandhill country, one hundred and twenty miles north-west of Barrow Creek. Had it not been for the attractions a young lady possessed for one of my boys, and the blandishments with which he wooed and won her, the locality of the well and the story connected with it might never have been known. His home was in that desolate, well-watered country, but the young lady's presence held him in Barrow Creek.

Being there I heard of the snake from this boy, and took him to show me the waters on my first journey from Barrow Creek to Victoria River. As stated elsewhere, our equipment consisted of twenty camels, four whites, and two native boys. On the way he spoke of the beautiful springs of fresh water that existed in his country, and in one was this snake. He was a monster that could easily swallow a man. But if left in peace, and if the water in which he dwelt was used in moderation, and dipped out quietly, the snake raised no objection.

Wattle (or Snake) Well lies a few miles south-east of Giant Well. A ring of *Gastrolobium* poison-bush country surrounds the hollow, in which there is grazing for camels. The floor of the hollow, about five or six square miles in area, is a flat expanse of firm sand, bare flat floors of travertine-limestone, and samphire-covered ground that in heavy rain forms swamps, with water in them up to a foot deep. At such times countless swimming or wading birds find food there.

After traversing many miles of tumbled sand and sandhills - with the camels' jaws lashed together with nose-line cord to prevent them taking bites of the deadly *Gastrolobium* bushes through which they have to travel - rather suddenly the hollow opens out before one. A great and very welcome change from the closely hemmed in valleys; you feel the vivifying effect of open space as you pass down the slope. The sage green of the samphire swamps, and the bright emerald green of the wattles ahead fills one with the expectancy of a pleasant camp.

Our boy piloted the string to near the water, pointed in the direction in which it lay, and said it was only a short distance within the patch of wattles. This variety of wattle is a good indication in that country of water near the surface.

An inspection of the spot revealed a round hole, some three feet in diameter, in a flat floor of limestone. Beneath the floor, which was only a foot or eighteen inches thick, the hole extended back in every direction, like an inverted funnel, and over the whole floor of the well extended a bright sheet of water. The prospect seemed encouraging for a drink for the camels, so we made camp beyond spear-throw-length from the edge of the wattle, boiled a pot of tea, and prepared to test the yield of water in the well. Half a dozen buckets showed that the well needed cleaning out. There was, as is always the case with native wells, much black, shining mud, sand, and decaying leaves in it, as well as the remains of all the birds, lizards, and small marsupials that had been drowned in it. Fortunately the water was as fresh as rain-water. After twenty camels had been satisfied, the water would be pure enough for us.

So far the snake had not been mentioned by either blacks or whites. As we were there ready to clean out the well, I told the boys that we (they and I) would take It in turns to fill the buckets in the well while the others hauled it out and carried it well away. The sludge was of the consistency and colour of discoloured pea soup.

Now, in all my dealings with the natives through many years, I never asked a native to do anything I was not prepared, if necessity arose, to do myself. The boys were very reluctant to get down into the hole. I knew that they were not afraid of the mud; they have to clean out dirty soakage waters every day. So I asked the principal boy why they hesitated. He told me plainly that the great snake had his home in the bottom of the hole; he indicated with his hands where, and said:

"If I get down there he will bite me."

I thereupon got a long stick, probed every possible place where it might be lurking, and by moving the stick rapidly to and fro satisfied myself that no snake was there. (I was satisfied before I started.) A practical demonstration was the only thing to convince them, so I stripped off and jumped into the well. Their eyes were like great saucers as I did so. They watched intently until the bulk of the filthy mass (probably the accumulation of centuries) was emptied out and the bottom of the stinking pit began to show.

My companions then began to ask the boys all sorts of questions, and turned the whole tale into ridicule, then and on many occasions thereafter. Personally I refrained from wounding the boys' feelings more than could be helped, and seldom referred to the matter. They are sensitive to ridicule; and to have the story that had been related to them so often by the fathers of the tribe knocked on the head was a severe blow to their credulity. But there was no help for it. We needed water for the camels; and fresh water and fair grazing in safety from the deadly *Gastrolobium* at the same camp were of great worth to us at that time.

Tradition records that in the beginning there were forefathers who belonged to the Rain Totem, and to the Clouds Totem and that these Rain-Totem Men possessed sacks, in which were stored thunder, lightning, hail, and rain in unlimited quantities. Occasionally these Rain Men, alone or in company, would ascend into the heavens, open their sacks, and pour out thunder, lightning, rain and so forth to any extent they saw fit. When they had finished their mission on earth they turned their bodies into rocks and trees, and their souls returned to the cave under the earth from which they originally came.

Rain dance at Charlotte Waters, 1895.

In these later times when rain is wanted the sorcerers get busy and bring rain as follows: if the rain-stone is rubbed the rain-man comes out of the earth, goes up into the sky and empties out his rain-sack. His bellowing or booming is the thunder. The natives say, *"Kwatja angama"* (the Water Man speaks). They have in mind that one of the original Rain-Totem Forefathers bas been apprised by the rubbing of the stone that rain is wanted on earth, that he has gone up into the heavens and is pouring some thunder from his sack. The thunder being his voice, they naturally say, "The Water Man speaks."

One would expect the natives to be terrified at the awe-inspiring spectacle some of the Central Australian thunder-storms present at times. They are not. When the thunder rends the air in deafening claps, and the lightning is playing around in blinding zigzags, and feels dangerously near, the natives show no fear. On the contrary, they will converse freely, make light of it, and even burst out laughing at an unusually loud, or peculiar clap of thunder.

The worst thunder-storm I ever experienced was at the Woodforde Well, about forty miles south of Central Mount Stuart. I had four working boys with me at the time, and we had let the camels go for the night.

The evening was close and sultry; not a breath of wind rustled the leaves of the gum-trees along the creek. Otherwise there was nothing to indicate that a storm was approaching. Soon a rumbling of distant thunder came from the west, and the clouds in that direction reflected the lightning from a storm still below the horizon. Presently, and in nearly every direction, the outline of cumuli appeared on the horizon, and here and there in advance of the wool packs were small dense clouds.

The sky was still clear of clouds above, but the rumbling of distant thunder, and the play of lightning in every cloud was ominous. I deemed it wise to prepare for heavy rain. The camp equipment was placed on the high-water mark of former Woodforde floods. We had made things safe and finished our evening meal about sundown. The sky by that time was covered with, shall I say, a blending of cirrus and cumulus clouds, an arrangement that often precedes rain in that part. The clouds were flying hither and thither, the different layers apparently finding no retarding clouds in the courses they were bent on following.

Then from the west a bank of black cloud arose like a pall; in and about it there was not a moment's cessation of the play of lightning, and the brighter flashes were the signal for terrific thunder-claps. To stay where we were - under the gum-trees seemed like courting disaster; so I called to the boys to come with me to higher and more open ground. They came readily enough, and for half an hour or more the play of lightning around us, and the fearful claps of thunder just above our heads made one feel one was in the midst of a raging titanic battle. It was very terrible, but at the same still very grand.

Yet the boys laughed and joked through it all; showed neither admiration nor fear. To them, it was just the Rain Man up aloft emptying out his bag of tricks.

Arrernte men with body painted for *Illionpa* corroboree
(public ceremony for entertainment), Alice Springs, 1896.

8

PUNISHMENTS TO FIT THE CRIME

MISDEEDS, misdemeanours and offences - often pure superstitious conceptions - are sometimes dealt with in the most savage and brutal way. At others the culprit is let off lightly, the punishment being toned down in severity largely by the number and fighting capabilities of the culprit's near relatives.

A recognized rule is that when a woman marries a man she becomes his absolute property, with the right to treat her as his slave, and to beat her as he likes until she conforms to his wishes. Relatives rarely interfere; when they do, several join in and the issue may be a battle royal.

Many women, and most of the youths, live in fear of the old men, whose word is law i and summary punishment is administered in the form of a hard blow with the first stick that can be laid hands on. I remember a case in point that happened at Connor Well, on the Overland Telegraph Line, when a large party of whites were camped there.

One evening we heard great wailing in the natives' camp, so we went over to see what had happened. On the ground was a woman apparently dead, with bleeding wounds on her head and body. One of the natives had for some reason or other, beaten her until she fell insensible. Some fifty yards away a great commotion was going on. One native, a relative of the woman, spear in hand upraised, was trying to get a shot at the culprit, and about twenty others, all armed with spears, were dodging in and out and thereby keeping the two apart. Had he not been prevented the relative would either have killed, or been killed; for he was in deadly earnest, thinking the woman had been killed. She, however, much to every one's surprise, gradually regained consciousness, at which the excitement as gradually cooled down, and nothing further occurred on that occasion.

I was camped at Henbury station in the early days, when Tempe Downs station was being formed. I had not then become used to the barbarous modes of punishment that the natives sometimes practise on their wives. A young lubra, probably not more than sixteen years old, was supposed to have offended her lord and master in some way or other. He went to the kitchen, and asked the cook for the loan of a butcher's knife, and also asked him to sharpen it. Quite innocently the cook sharpened it and gave it to him. The next we knew was that the lubra had a frightful gash across the thigh that would leave a scar six inches long to her dying day.

Ten years afterwards a mob of Henbury blacks was camped not far from my own camp at Charlotte Waters Telegraph Station. I walked over to see them, and while there asked if the woman that had been slashed with a butcher's knife was among them. The other women pointed to one in the group; she bared her thigh and showed a dreadful scar.

The road from the Missionaries down the Finke does not enter the Glen of Palms. It skirts the ranges to Ellery's Creek, follows that watercourse to its confluence with the Finke, and so on through the ranges. My caravan had left the Missionaries and camped that night at Ellery's Creek, where a girl about fifteen years old had arranged to accompany my boys' lubras to Henbury station, sixty miles farther south. Next morning as we entered the Ellery's Creek Gorge I heard dreadful screams, and then all was still. My blacks ran to a thicket and found the girl prone with blood running from great wounds on her head and shoulders. She had been thrashed with a boomerang until she fell senseless, by a man to whom she had been promised.

My blacks got her round and helped her along to the Finke. There the heat overpowered her, and she staggered and fell. We gave her water to drink, put her upon one of the camels and took her to the next camp. In the morning she was all swollen lumps and scars, and quite unable to walk, so we again put her on a camel and in due course delivered her to her own people.

Real conjugal happiness, as we understand it, is foreign to the natives, except perhaps in rare cases. Chastity and fidelity are unknown; the only sin in sexual indulgence with some other man belonging to her proper marrying-class is in her being found out. The woman listens to the blandishments of some young man during interviews obtained by stealth, with the result that he surreptitiously runs away with her.

This stealing and running off with some other fellow's wife is a favourite pastime with the natives, and few of them are without scars on their bodies obtained while the rightful owner of the woman administers cuts and stabs with a stone knife by way of compensation for the injustice done to him..

A husband, finding his wife gone, follows up her tracks and, if fortunate enough to overtake the eloping couple, at once demands satisfaction from the man, who may elect to be cut about to his pursuer's satisfaction. The cuts are usually in the region of the shoulder blades; but the position seems to be optional with the aggrieved party.

The woman may get a terrible thrashing or be let off scot-free, according to her explanation as to whether she was a consenting party or not.

Or it may be that the man, if he be a good fighter, may think his cuts too deep or too many. In that case he may elect to fight for the woman, and if he wins she is his. Or he may decide to fight for the woman before he is cut, but if he wins he mayor may not be allowed to keep her altogether unless - the elders in council permit him to do so.

Elopement, free or forced, with a man from another tribe is of frequent occurrence; there are many instances on record where a wife ran away with someone in her own tribe also. The following is one that came under my notice. While we were camped at Connor Well, groups of blacks from two or three tribes were also camped there; and as they drew their supplies of water from the well, none other being available within several miles, we got to know most of them by sight. Among them were two women.

Single, unattached, and pregnant women camp by themselves in the women's camp (*lukara*), and these two were the only ones occupying it.

Early one morning they were missing. Two blackfellows, who had come in from the north quite recently, were also away. The other natives found by their tracks that the two men from the north had gone to the lukara and taken the two women, willy-nilly, to the head of the Woodforde Creek, then westward towards the Lander. Up to the time I left the district, some months after-wards, the women had not been heard of.

When called upon in this way the women have to go or be killed. As a rule I fancy they take it very philosophically, being rather proud to be the recipients of special attention. Perhaps, too, upon their return the retailing of their experiences makes them the envy of their less fortunate sisters.

While camped at the Winnecke mining-centre I learned of another instance. Several Barrow Creek natives, of the Katitja tribe, came there on a visit and were hospitably treated by the local tribe. One morning the wife of one of the working boys was missing. The boy at the time had been sent on some mission to Alice Springs, fifty miles away. When he returned he was furious, and tried to borrow a rifle with which to be avenged. Whether he was successful I do not remember; but after many days he returned, much crest-fallen. He had done his best to overtake his wife, having first rid himself of boots and clothes. In leaving his boots behind he had made a great mistake. The elopers had taken a route that led over rough stony ground, infested with three-cornered jacka - a very bad prickle. When the boy came to travel over this, with feet that had grown soft by wearing boots for years, he was at a great disadvantage; he soon got footsore; had to admit to himself that he was beaten, and finally returned without his wife.

Several months afterwards the abductor and the stolen wife came to Alice Springs with a travelling mob of cattle. The woman was allowed to remain there and her former husband took her back, as though nothing had happened.

This lady must have been full of charm. The Winneeke boy first stole her from someone at Arltunga. She was then stolen, as above related, by a Barrow Creek native. After being taken back to Winnecke, she again ran away (or was taken) to Arltunga. Finally she was once more brought to Winnecke by him who was considered by the natives there to be her rightful owner. So far as I heard, he never ill-treated her upon her return.

With other elopements that came under my notice things did not run nearly so smoothly. A native was employed at the Mount Charlotte Well on the Mount Burrell (now Maryvale) cattle station to draw water, for which he used a pair of quiet bullocks in an appliance called a whip. He was assisted by three wives who drove the bullocks and landed the bucket in turns. If I remember rightly, he had still another wife working at an outstation called Alice Well. However, of the three he had with him one had been stolen by him from another blackfellow in early life; she was weather-worn, wrinkly, and old. Another was also past the meridian. The third was young and much treasured by him.

One day a young blackfellow was seen speaking to her. Later in the day, when the incident was forgotten by the young fellow, the old man gave him a blow with a stick that laid him up for several days. Undaunted by this intimation of what lay in store for him he still persisted in paying addresses to the young wife, surreptitiously of course. The wiles of a young lover proved too attractive in the end, and she eloped with him to Deep Well.

The old man, who was a great warrior, tracked them up and, coming upon her unexpectedly while surrounded by several others, took her by the wrist (the young lover being absent at the time), led her away a few yards from the crowd, then hit her across the small of the back with a boomerang, which felled her to the ground. He then took her to the natives' camp and throughout the evening and night kept deriding her and prodding her with the point of a spear. These proddings were simply barbarous; the poor thing suffered agonies.

In the morning she was scarcely able to walk, but he bundled her along before him back on the road she had come. When over the first sandhill, about half a mile, he ordered a halt and there watched for the return to the camp of the young man who had stolen her.

This the young fellow did after a while, thinking the old warrior had left for good. Settling himself down among his pals he listened to an account of what had happened during his absence, and thanked his lucky stars that the old man had not seen him. Before all that had happened had been related to him, to his amazement there stood the old warrior, spear poised and all, standing in front of him. Jumping up, he tried to dodge, but the old man drove his spear through the young buck's leg, which crippled him for a month or two. Then the old warrior took his wife back to Mount Charlotte.

Fierce fights for a woman are sometimes waged, in which friends or relatives take a hand if they see that the battle is going against their protagonist. While I was camped at Ryan's Well on one occasion a young, finely-built native arrived from Alice Springs and demanded from an older, but much smaller man, the return of his lubra whom the smaller man had stolen. The lady was unwilling. It was finally arranged that the two should fight for her, and the victor take her.

Next morning, armed with as many boomerangs as could be mustered, the combatants faced each other at good throwing distance. The battle waxed stronger and stronger, and the space between the fighters grew less and less. The friends of each quickly picked up the weapons and handed them to their man. After a while it became evident that the smaller man was the better fighter, and the friends of the younger saw fit to help him. This brought help to the other side. Lubras screamed and knives were called for. A melee ensued, in which the large man was frightfully cut about, the smaller man also being badly handled. A warrior, a boy whom we were employing in our camp, thinking to help his friend, rushed into the thick of it near the end of the combat, He came back with a cut on his thigh four inches long and one inch deep.

On another occasion while camped at Ryan's Well for the night I had an exciting experience, through the indiscretion of two of my boys. I had four boys with me at the time, forty-five camels, ten tons of loading, and a four-hundred-mile journey still in front of me. The boys were sent out as usual for the camels at daylight; they were not brought back until midday, which meant a late start. The boys were given their food and, the sun being strong, they took it to the shade of a tree a few yards beyond the saddles. I was preparing to have my meal also when, apparently from nowhere, two painted natives appeared. They were heavily armed with spears and other weapons and held their beards in their mouths. They came straight for me.

For a moment things looked very serious; my rifle was attached to my saddle and there was no time to get it. However, they strode quickly past me to where my boys were eating their meal. The two younger boys immediately jumped up and dodged, but a spear grazed the leg of one of them and went through his trousers. The other boy, with his butcher's knife in his hand, ran behind me dodging from side to side all the time to prevent the warrior from getting a sure shot at him with his spear. He knew that the blackfellow would hesitate before spearing me.

Fortunately I recognized the warrior. He was a man I had known for years, who always looked me up when passing and never failed to get a meal and a little tobacco; in fact we were very good friends. Clearly, the two boys had been misconducting themselves and deserved to be punished. Speaking to him kindly I induced him to put down his spear. I told him I had no objection to my boys being punished if they had done wrong; but it they lamed or disabled them then I could not possibly deliver my load; if they would postpone dealing with them until my return I would give them food and tobacco. To this he agreed, and signalled to his mate, whom my two older boys had managed to pacify somewhat, to come over to me. I then gave both of them what I had promised and they went back to their camp.

It turned out that my two younger boys, knowing the old men's wives would take the local mob of sheep and goats out to graze all day, instead of going after the camels stopped behind where the flock of sheep would be shepherded, and there awaited the arrival of the lubras. When the two honest boys brought back the whole mob of camels the scamps joined up with them and walked into the camp as bold as brass, thinking I would never know. Nor would I but for the above happening. The two warriors evidently suspected, and kept a watch from a distance, and because of what they saw they decided to punish the boys by laming each with a spear.

Some purloiners of women have to pay very dearly for them. Stealing other men's wives is by no means confined to the young unmarried men; the married men sometimes steal other men's wives. One culprit was a boy I kept in my employ all the time I was trying to find a stock-route between the centre of the continent and Victoria River. I employed him for his special knowledge of the country that lies north-west of Barrow Creek. That was his country. Like so many of the outback natives, he had come in to Barrow Creek to see for himself what the much-talked-about white men were like. This was some years before I employed him.

While at Barrow Creek he paid his addresses to an unattached young lady and induced her to elope with him. After several months of honeymooning on the lower Hanson Creek they quarrelled and, while he was away hunting one day, she ran back to Barrow Creek. He followed her up and induced her to live with him again, and they had been living together in her own (Barrow Creek) country up to the time he came to work for me. He was very green at camel work, but a superb tracker.

We started out to cross the stretch between Barrow Creek and Victoria River, a distance of more than three hundred miles, which till then was thought to be waterless. In addition to that boy we took another to help him hunt the camels in the mornings. Two hundred miles out from Barrow Creek the two boys bolted one night, and returned to Barrow Creek. That necessitated our hunting up the camels ourselves for the rest of the way to Victoria River and back to Barrow Creek.

On the next trip through to Victoria River I induced the same boy to accompany me, and arranged for him to bring his lubra, thinking he might not run away if she accompanied him. For further security a friend of his and the friend's lubra also were taken along. They did not run away that time. Back at Barrow Creek the boy's services were dispensed with.

The next I heard of him was that he had been stabbed all over with a stone knife, and lay at death's door. I was then raising wolfram at the Wauchope mining-field, about eighty miles north of Barrow Creek; and the stabbing had taken place only three or four miles from my camp. His lubra came over and begged some food to give him. This I gave her, and told her to bring him to me when he was well enough to move.

After several days they came. I found he had been stabbed with a short stone knife in eighteen or twenty places on the chest, and shoulders to the armpits. How the lungs escaped permanent injury is a mystery; he had great difficulty in breathing and suffered much pain with it. He finally recovered.

Now for the story! I closely questioned both the boy and his lubra as to how and why the stabbing happened. While they were camped at the Wycliffe Well, some twenty miles south of the Wauchope, the boy had become enamoured of another man's wife - a young lubra. The boy told his wife to bring the lubra to his camp. Knowing his intentions, she refused to do so. The upshot was that the boy ran away with the other fellow's wife. They made for a very rocky part in the Davenport Ranges, to a spot four or five miles east of where I was camped. Fixing on a very secluded spot in which to camp, in a thicket, and feeling secure from their pursuers for that night at any rate, they went to sleep.

The next thing the boy knew was that he was in the firm grip of half a dozen men. They dragged him out into the open, stood him up, and held him fast while the husband of the woman with whom he had run away stabbed him until he had had satisfaction. They had tracked the runaways, saw where they made their camp, and gave them time to get to sleep before pouncing on them.

A peculiar ruling in this case was arrived at by the old men in council. It was decided that the punishment meted out to the thief did not fit the crime; it was altogether too severe; for that reason the stabber had to give up his wife (the stolen woman) to the man he had stabbed. That ruling points to the small value the natives place on a woman; she is regarded as a chattel, and a few stabs is her price. The boy had paid more than the full price for his second wife.

But there is a sequel. Not-withstanding that the first wife did more than the second to save his life, when he recovered she decided to leave him for his faithlessness. A young strong man saw that she was discontented and paid his addresses, and her husband let her go. They had not been living together very long when they disagreed. The young fellow then knocked her down, kicked her insensible, and left her there. Other women then nursed her back to life, and fed her to convalescence, when her former husband took her back. After that the two wives agreed much better.

The natives have social customs that carry almost as much weight as definite rules or commands. One is that a blackfellow should not go to camps or grounds where women are congregated. It is not considered decorous for a man to intrude on their privacy. More especially is this the case if some of the women belong to men who object to him. I am not referring to clandestine visits but open brazen approaches. The following shows how strongly that kind of behaviour is resented:

For some reason unknown to me I was asked to take with me for a couple of trips a police tracker stationed at Oodnadatta. He went by the European name of Bendigo. Now Bendigo had been much with the whites, and could talk English fluently. Being a police officer he thought the natives would not dare to molest him; to impress them with his importance he put on much swagger. I warned him on different occasions along the road not to be so reckless in going to the camps without being invited or escorted by the men. As we stayed only a night at each camping-place I succeeded in returning him to his employer without mishap, and was glad to be rid of the responsibility.

Bendigo evidently carried on the same practices at Oodnadatta for my boys told me that he had been warned by other natives of the risks he ran. As time wore on he grew more and more reckless, and the natives decided among themselves to put an end to it. The Neales watercourse is about two miles from Oodnadatta, and Bendigo was invited there to an evening's entertainment. While the corroboree was in full swing the natives fell upon and beat the life out of him. In the morning the blackfellow who shepherded the sheep for the local butcher was seen to have much blood about him. When he was questioned, the fact leaked out that Bendigo had been murdered.

The reason for the blood on the shepherd was that he had carried the lifeless body all the way from the corroboree ground to near the Oodnadatta artesian bore, where he threw it down and left it.

Bendigo having travelled with my boys, they were much interested in his fate. It was just punishment for his unseemly conduct, they said.

9

HOW THE WOMEN SETTLE THEIR LITTLE DIFFERENCES

IN their normal primitive state a woman's portion is to provide her lord and master with ground-up seeds, edible roots, fruit, grubs, lizards, snakes, rats, in short anything edible that comes her way; and to cook it if it needs cooking, make the camp comfortable, and get wood and water.

She is a valuable asset, and the man who can obtain, and retain, two, three, or four wives can spend most of his time in a leisurely fashion, without having to exert himself much in hunting for big game. If the food is not there at the appointed time, he does not hesitate to administer such verbal and physical correction as will prevent a repetition of his empty stomach. And no one has any right to remonstrate, for she is to all intents and purposes his slave.

Some husbands are more lenient than others: but every native considers it necessary to keep his women "well under the whip." In a servile way the wife does her husband's bidding, his wishes being always in the form of a command. That being so it is difficult to understand what now follows:

The cause of the women's quarrels more often than not lies in the attempt - real or supposed - of some other woman to decoy a husband from the path of virtue, and incidentally from the aggrieved party. The accusation is made and, very naturally, hotly resented; much reciprocal slander follows; the choicest billingsgate is thrown, until the opposing parties' thighs quiver, their bodies shake and tremble, and their mouths foam with rage. They will stand and harangue one another for some time; secrets that in the ordinary way would never be divulged are made public. Goaded to desperation they now rush for any fighting-sticks that are about; if none are to hand they rush for their yam-sticks (*atnama*) and away to the nearest open space.

There they become more guarded, cease talking and calm themselves. As they slowly close one is seen to hold her stick horizontally well above her head with the two hands near the ends of the stick. This is done to guard the head against the blows her opponent will deliver. They do not thrust; it is all a matter of striking blows from above. They may be quick in succession, but not always vertical.

The art of self-defence lies in placing the guard to intercept the blow at an angle near the right-angle, otherwise the striking stick glides along the guard, and the fingers of the woman on the defensive are broken. She can then neither guard off the blows of her antagonist nor inflict them herself, with the consequence that her head and shoulders get beaten about in a way that would certainly kill a white woman.

Usually, two women thus in combat take turn and turn about at striking and guarding if they be evenly matched; but a good fighter will sometimes feint guarding, then with lightning rapidity start striking before her opponent is ready with her guard.

While a fight is in progress the other women who happen to be in camp, taking sides, yell and scream. When blood flows freely, and fingers and heads are broken, they behave more like fiends than human beings, and the camp is bedlam. The men in the camp, including the husbands, simply look on, or go on talking to one another with perfect indifference. To them it is "only a women's row!" and the women must settle their own quarrels. It is beneath the dignity of a man to interfere.

But let the wife taunt the husband ever so little and she is likely to receive punishment in a form she will not soon forget. I was engaged on certain work at the Stirling station, near Barrow Creek, when one of the station lubras was speared through the leg by her husband, one of the working boys. I went over and asked the woman about the affray.

"It was all my fault," she said. "I wouldn't shut up when he told me to, so he speared me in the leg."

I asked another lubra about it, and she said:

"You know, Kopra Koolta [that was her name] is a b-- to talk. She wouldn't shut up when Tjippi [her husband's name, and short for Tjubearta] told her to; so he speared her. It was all her fault."

I told Tjippi he would have to go to jail. He replied:

"I suppose I'll have to. But she wouldn't shut up."

The native is a puzzle as regards his mentality. He can be extremely brutal and at the same time extremely kind. An instance of each will show what I mean. I was returning from one of my long trips, having delivered a load of stores to Newcastle Waters. The season was a dry one. South Newcastle Waters was nearly dry, and one of the camels had ventured too far into the mud that surrounded the last drop of water in the large waterhole. So we fixed the harness on the draught camel we had trained to draw water from the wells along the telegraph line, tied ropes about the bogged animal, and hauled him out on to dry land.

When we reached Renners Springs, half a dozen cattle were bogged there, so we hauled them out with the same camel - a very powerful animal - by fastening a rope to their horns. Now, bush cattle are safe enough in a bog, but when you drag them to firm ground, the first thing they do is to charge you, and if you are not quick in getting out of the road they may toss you. So we devised a slip-knot on the rope and, as soon as they were landed and before they had time to get on their feet, we had reached a tree or some other safe cover. The four boys I had with me had not been amiable to one another for some unknown reason; one was quarrelsome. This came out more prominently a few days later when, to get water at Attack Creek, we were obliged to travel through a dense thicket to reach a waterhole four or five miles farther down the creek than the usual watering-place, which was then dry. So we had to camp late. I overheard the other boys telling the quarrelsome one to "shut up. " Nothing further occurred until we reached a camp called the Glue Pot some five miles south of Ryan's Well.

It was evening. The camels had been turned out to graze; the boys had finished their evening meal, and were sitting on the saddles about twenty yards from where I was repairing one. No unusual raising of voices was heard. Things appeared to be quite normal when suddenly the discontented boy sprang to his feet, gathered up his boomerangs, a heavy nulla-nulla (a lubra's fighting-stick) and a shield; ran to my portable table, seized one of my butcher's knives, placed it in his belt, and hurried out thirty or forty yards from the saddles, calling loudly to the youngest of the boys to get his fighting equipment, which consisted of a shield and three boomerangs only.

He was really no match for the older man, and apparently saw no occasion to fight; but being thus challenged to open combat he had no option but to do the best he could. He did not even go out from the saddles, but stood not far from the other boys. The elder man started throwing his boomerangs at a great pace. and the younger responded. These were either dodged or parried by both parties, By the time all the boomerangs were thrown the elder man was already facing the younger among the saddles, and with the nulla-nulla in one hand, and shield in the other, was dealing smashing blows at the head of the youth, who successfully parried them until his shield broke in pieces.

That of course settled his chance of evading the blows; the next one came smashing down on the top of his head, leaving him dazed and powerless. His antagonist then dropped his shield; took both hands to the nulla-nulla; stepped to the side of the youth and hit him over the back of the head a very hard blow, which felled him like a log. As he stood over the apparently lifeless body I said:

"I think you have killed him; but get some water and bathe his head; if not dead you must bring him round if you can."

He seemed then to realize the serious thing he had done, and went for the water. Assisted by the other two boys he bathed the battered boy for

Aboriginal woman from the Arrernte tribe near Alice Springs, 1901.

hours on end. Towards midnight, to my great surprise, the lad regained semi-consciousness, and by morning showed signs that he might recover. We did not shift camp until he was well enough to hold his balance on a camel, then by short stages we got him along until he recovered.

How his skull withstood the blow is a mystery, for the fighting-stick was made of mulga (*Acacia aneura*), a very hard and heavy wood. The skulls of the natives must be very strong.

During my second journey across from Barrow Creek to Victoria River I witnessed a sight that only occurs on very rare occasions, namely, that of a woman, forbidden by the marriage code to go near or speak to a man that belongs to a certain marrying-class, throwing all restrictions to the winds and acting as nurse to him out of pure sympathy for the sick.

My party included my black boy and his lubra, and a friend of his, with his lubra. It was the middle of summer when we set out and the culmination of a long, severe drought, during which the Hanson and Lander creeks had not been flooded for five and seven years respectively. The end of the drought was approaching and the heat, as is usually the case at such times, was terrific and increased as we proceeded. When we had covered rather over two-thirds of the way, and were within a day's journey of Winnecke Creek, the incident happened. The water we carried on the camels was getting low, and we were all anxious as to how the waterholes in Winnecke Creek were standing the excessive heat.

My boy's friend was a warrigal, that is, he could neither speak nor understand any English; neither could his lubra. He had not learned to ride a camel and always did the day's journey on foot which, in ordinary weather, was child's play to him. But the terrific heat that day must have given him a slight sunstroke, although he was supplied with sundry drinks on the way. Upon our halting for the night's camp the poor fellow struggled to the shade of a tree, lay down at full length on his back and swooned. The lubras became greatly concerned, as did my boy.

The latter's lubra was strongly taboo to the sick man, and had no right to go near him, as the others well knew. Her sympathy for the sick, however, overcame all taboo restrictions; she deliberately went to him and bathed his head until he came round. Then, as deliberately, she got up and walked away, and to my knowledge never spoke to him during the rest of the journey to Victoria River and back to Barrow Creek - over five hundred miles.

The day after we reached Barrow Creek it started to rain, and continued until the creeks overflowed their banks, and all the lowlands became quagmires. At such times the natives head off the kangaroos towards the lowlands, run them until exhausted, then kill them with spear or boomerang.

Even when in the employ of Europeans, the boys are shy at passing through country belonging to other tribes, and for safety keep a sharp look out, especially if some old grievance is still unrequited. They may, and often do when on the border, decamp in the middle of the night rather than take the risk; and it is surprising how quickly they will be back at their starting-point. This fear of foul play is sometimes not without reason, as the following account will show: I once had two Europeans in my employ, sinking the Woodforde Well, on the Woodforde Creek; and one of them had brought a most useful and civilized native from Barrow Creek to tend his horses. The Woodforde and Teatree wells natives, for several years after the Barrow Creek tragedy occurred, were considered unreliable. As, however, their behaviour had been fairly satisfactory for some years past, although somewhat arrogant at times, they had not been molested. At the time the well was being sunk many Woodforde natives were camped in the neighbourhood, three or four of them with their wives being camped in the creek near where the work was going on.

At first the Barrow Creek native was shy, and always slept close to his master's tent, for he knew of some old grievance that awaited settlement. The natives showed their wish to be friendly by entertaining him with songs at night; presenting him with a spear or two, and in other ways as well. He became quite friendly and trusted them. They suggested to him one day that they all take their spears and go into the mountains and have a few hours sport, hunting wallabies. The plan was agreed to, and the four of them went off one morning.

Now, short gulches, narrow in places, have been worn back into the ranges there and small creeks run through them. and join the Woodforde out in the plain. Following one of these small creeks the hunters reached the foothills. While passing through a defile one of the three Woodforde natives dropped his spear-thrower, as if by accident, and stepped aside for the Barrow Creek boy to get in front of him. Picking up the thing he had dropped the Woodforde native walked close behind the other and drove his spear right through him through back and chest.

The boy was missed at the camp, but no trace of him, or word of his fate, was forthcoming for some weeks. The truth was at length carried to his relatives and friends at Barrow Creek, and a mob of avengers came down. But the murderers bad made away south; so the balancing of accounts was postponed indefinitely. With the natives old scores have to be settled some time, the rule being an eye for an eye and a tooth for a tooth. It may be years before a favourable opportunity occurs; but sooner or later some Woodforde boy will be found done to death in the Barrow Creek country.

Feuds of this kind go on all the time between the different tribes, and that greatest of all horrors and decimators of the people, the avenging party, goes out and does some innocent person to death. For some time the Federal Government has been trying to stop the practice; but if we may judge by the number of murder cases that are being tried in the courts, not much headway is being made.

An Arrernte tribesman. Alice Springs, 1896.

10
BETROTHALS AND MARRIAGE CUSTOMS

NATIVE men of middle to advanced age are very cunning in the methods they adopt for getting wives in advance. They take time by the forelock, so to say, and ask the parents for a female child as soon as it is born; in some cases the request is made in advance, being conditional on the expected child being a girl. Usually, however, the request is made when the girl is still small. Such requests are invariably accompanied by gifts of some sort.

Strehlow has set out the method of betrothal of a boy to a girl-child among the western Loritja people, and states that it is somewhat later than with the Aranda, say between four and ten years. My own observations lead me to believe that instead of the betrothal being arranged for the son it is more often arranged for the man himself.

However, here it is: The youth's father, desirous of securing a wife for his son in the future, goes to a man who has a child-daughter and asks: "Are you agreeable that our children marry?" The father of the maiden answers:

"Yes, I am agreeable." Then he goes away and says to the lad: "You boy are my son-in-law and shall regard me as your father-in-law."

And the son's father says to his future daughter-in-law:

"Daughter-in-law, you shall always bring water to me!" Then the father of the girl says to his future son-in-law:

"O son-in-law, you let this girl grow up first before you take her to wife."

When the children are bigger, the lad makes his father-in-law a present of meat and weapons; and the girl presents her future father-in-law with plant food, and brings him fire and water.

When the marriage day has arrived, an elder brother or grandfather decorates the young man with a forehead-band, and a girdle under which a bunch of long bird-feathers is tucked, and across his breast and over his eyes he is painted with red stripes. The bride is decorated with red ochre and carries a crown made by winding a cord, with rat-tail tips attached, around her head. The bride then retires to the unmarried girls' camp, and the bridegroom to the unmarried men's camp. Later, the bridegroom, accompanied by relatives, goes quite close to the women's camp and halts. Then a relative of the bridegroom goes up to the bride, seizes her by the arm, and conducts her to the bridegroom, who says:

"Give me the woman; she belongs to me."

The relative then places the bride's and bridegroom's right hands together and says to them:

"You both shall remain together. O maiden leave not this man. You both take one another for ever; you belong together. If you run away from this man so shall we follow after you and spear you."

The young man then allows his wife to go out gathering plant food with the other women, while he goes out to hunt with the other men. The wife joins him at his camp and he gives her some meat to take to her mother where she remains the night. The second day passes like the first. But when she has delivered the meat to her mother she must return and stay with him.

It is probable, according to the same authority, that the class system of marriage in vogue with the southern Loritja was originally somewhat different from that they have now that the class relationships became modified and less rigorous, owing to influences that came from the north. Which marriage organization - the eight-class or the four-class - was the original, is unfortunately unknown. The latter obtains in the south, and the rule there is for a man to possess one wife only.

The southern Loritja, Strehlow says, have a most unusual custom. If the legitimate wife of a man has a grown daughter, and the wife dies, the widower has the right to marry his own daughter, or he can take his cousin, or his aunt, for a wife.

He also mentions that the women and big girls play a game of "Oracle-play" to find out who among them are fruitful women and who are not. The name of the game is *ilbamara*.[6] The game is said to have been played by married women of "the beginning" called *ilbamara* women, in opposition to the class of women who would not marry. These latter, as their name *alknarintja* [7] implies, deliberately turned away their eyes from men.

One of the boys whom the writer took with him became possessed of a wife through the death of a brother. Strehlow's remarks on the wooing and marriage of a widow are interesting: Such of them as are not very young are under a ban of silence for about a year; during that time they talk only through the medium of the sign language, and maintain a modest and reserved demeanour, breaking out now and again in lamentation, but in a monotone only. When the women go to gather plant foods, the elderly women accompany the widow, who by the way, has to marry the younger brother of the former husband. The elderly women remind the men at the evening camp-fire that the widow is to marry the younger brother and not another man.

On the following day she is decorated as a bride: a cord, to which rat-tail tips are fastened, is wound round and round her head; her body, face, and arms are painted with red lines; and she wears a nose-bone in her nose.

The bridegroom (the younger brother) paints his body with black and red stripes; draws a red stripe over his eyes; puts on a forehead-band and an armband; puts a bone through his nose; places a bunch of eagle-feathers upright under his girdle in the centre of his back, and rat-tail tips behind his ears.

Relatives then accompany the bridegroom to where the women are gathered together, and he takes his sister-in-law, who is now his wife, and the marriage is complete. The other men admonish the married couple to be constant to one another; the young man is threatened with deadly threats and the young woman is similarly warned by her sisters. Then the men go hunting, and the women collect seed. When the young married man returns, he finds his camp swept clean and is presented with already prepared plant food. He partitions out anything he may have caught and sends a part by his wife to his mother-in-law. Having fulfilled that mission she returns to him.

To prevent reprisals on the newly-married pair by avenging parties, the men assemble and make a big demonstration by painting themselves, wearing a small *wonninga* in the hair, and singing warlike and avenging songs. In the past whole camps of quite innocent persons have been wiped out by avenging parties. The natives are much in fear of them, and for good reason.

The idea of trial marriages is not altogether modern. From time immemorial it has obtained to some extent. The practice among the aborigines appears to be winked at, and thereby receives tacit approval. I have noticed it and have also been informed of it on many occasions, and under very different situations. The case now to be related is one of many; the actors largely belonged to my own camp.

As is well known, the natives have rules for the disposal of a deceased man's property. He may own a corroboree (the sole right to some totemic performance), or a wife, or spears and shields. A wife is one of his chattels, and upon her husband's decease she becomes the property of a younger brother. That younger brother is supposed to take her and her children even though he may already have one or more wives and children. If he does not wish to keep her, he may give her to some other man of his own marrying-class that may desire her.

One of my boys took charge of his deceased brother's widow and kept her under close surveillance for several months; he then handed her over to a tribal brother, together with her child.

For some time prior to the final "giving away" of this woman a condition of things obtained that may be described as "a trial marriage."

Sometimes during this period the woman was in one camp and sometimes in the other, the stays getting gradually longer in her future husband's camp each day until she spent the best part of her time there. Finally she stayed there altogether, the man to whom she fell as a legacy having given a somewhat tardy consent. As he already had a wife she may, through jealousy, have persuaded him to let her go.

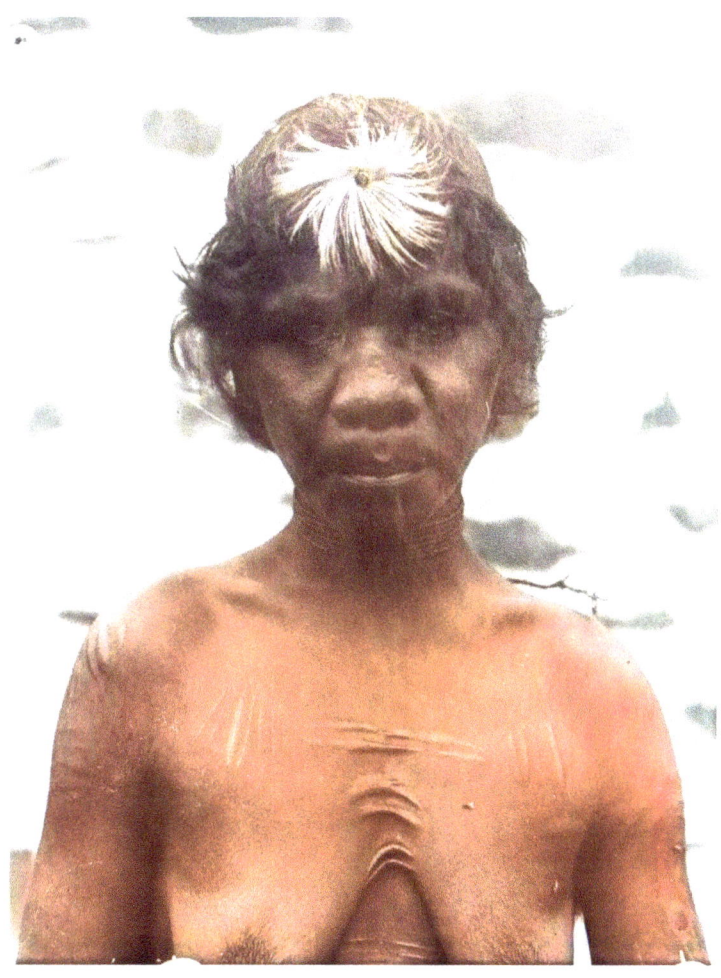

Kaititja woman wearing a decorated head-band and fur-string neck-ring. Ornamental scars show on her chest. Barrow Creek, 1901.

11
LENDING AND EXCHANGE OF WIVES

THE exchange of wives temporarily, and the lending of them to their friends, are customary; the latter in the ordinary course of things, the former in connexion with the performance of ceremonies. The woman has no say in the transaction: her part is to obey implicitly.

It is well known that certain men fail for years to get a wife apportioned to them. I asked one man whom I knew very well at the Stirling station, near Barrow Creek, why it was that he had no lubra, and how he got along without one. He told me that the old men had appropriated the young women he might have married. To help him out a friend of his occasionally lent him his wife.

"How does he get to know that you want her?" "I ask him for her. Sometimes he will lend her; sometimes he says he cannot."

There is no doubt that such matters are discussed among them with little or no reserve. This is not to be wondered at when one grasps the significance of their marriage code which apportions all the women in one of the eight marrying-classes as potential wives to the men in another of the classes. The woman this man asked for belonged to the class he should rightly select a wife from: she might have been his wife had his lucky star been in the ascendant. A man would not think of asking for the wife of another man if she belonged to a class taboo to him. It is not considered undignified for a friend to ask for the loan of a woman of the right class.

If a native wishes to treat his guest hospitably he will send a woman to his camp. The native boys working with caravans of camels save up their food, and in exchange for it a woman is sent to their camp for the night. In every case of lending women that came to my knowledge some little consideration, in the way of food, tobacco, or clothes, was invariably paid.

The natives' way of love-making reminds one that Solomon, with all his wisdom, could not understand the way of a man with a maid; it is questionable whether he could do so today - so far, at least, as these natives are concerned. How the sexes endear themselves to each other is something of a mystery to the whites. That much love-making goes on among them is certain. That the advances made are mutual is equally certain, not-withstanding strict rules of etiquette whereby the young men and women do not mix indiscriminately; have in fact to keep at speaking distance; and that the girls are rigidly chaperoned by the old women, and the young men by the old men.

They resort to surreptitious methods of communication. I have frequently noted that some juvenile has been made the medium by which a little food, or some trifling adornment for the person, is presented to the lady with whom a youth is enamoured. At other times I have known them. bribe some woman relative to convey the present, and some message.

Once on familiar terms the only thing that efficaciously restrains an eager couple is the enforcement of the marriage code rules, coupled with the caustic vituperation of the old women. These possess a vocabulary of choice billingsgate that often can shame even the shameless. The further stage (very often taken nowadays) is to make a bolt of it and chance the consequences.

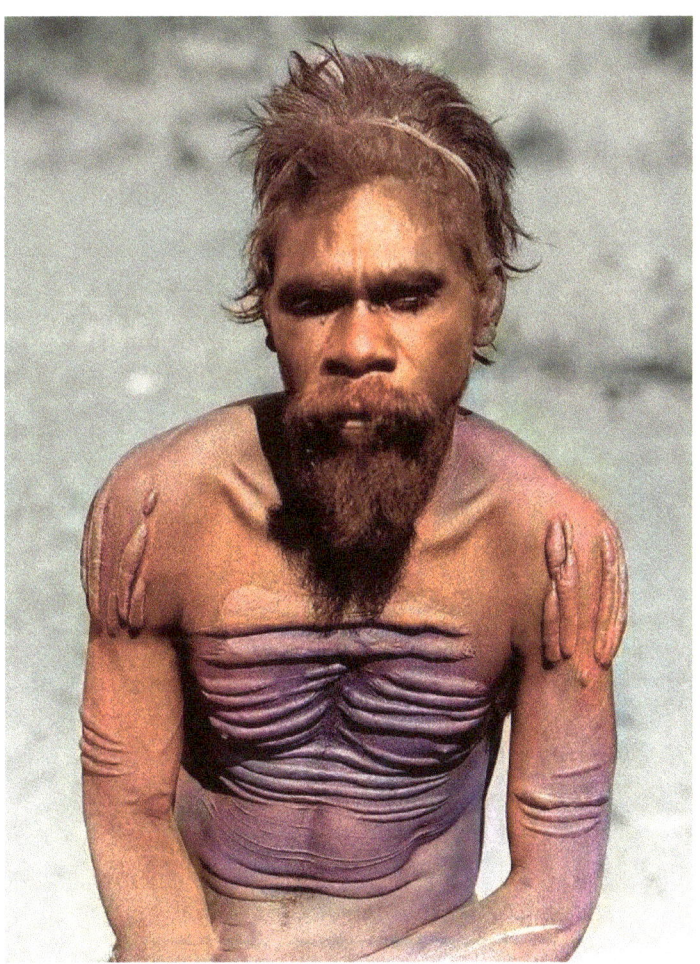

Tjingili man with well-marked cicatrices. Powell Creek, 1901.

12
CICATRICES AND MUTILATIONS

THE raised lines of skin that every native grown to mature state appears to possess may, in some cases or in some parts, have status or tribal significance; more often they appear to be purely marks of adornment. These cicatrices or keloids are made to run horizontally as a rule, one below the other across the chest, abdomen, shoulders, or arms. Those across the chest they call *urbma*, and those across the abdomen *imbulkna*. Some of these rolls of skin are as thick as one's little finger; others about the diameter of a lead pencil.

Strehlow ascertained from the natives that the weals are developed in the following way, which corresponds with my own observations: A slight incision is first made in the skin and filled with sand. This is not allowed to heal, being broken open from time to time and more sand put in. In nature's efforts to heal, the skin thickens, and so these cord-like weals are formed.

A painful process, and a good deal of time is taken up in its development. They are artistically placed and seldom out of alignment. An incision, say one inch long, is first made, and this is lengthened at alternate ends while the other end is healing; thereby an inch of sore is kept going for months at a stretch.

The natives are evidently proud of these cicatrices, and willingly undergo the pain and inconvenience of the sores while they are being developed.

Bedaubing the hair with grease and ochre is a common practice. They are fond of anointing the body with grease. I have seen them stand in the sun and rub the grease into the skin. But they will not travel far in the hot sun with only grease on their skin: it is too hot, so they rub the grease off with dirt. Red ochre is often mixed with the grease before rubbing it into the skin. The mixture makes the skin shine. It also binds together the strands of their hair. These they separate into pendants like so many pencils hanging down. The natives have several different ways of doing up the hair. Some shape it into rolls.

The George Gills Range natives (as stated in the chapter "Training Young Fighters") bedaub the hair copiously, draw it straight back from the forehead and head generally, and bind it round many times with string so that it stands straight out behind. With the addition of a white forehead-band that ties behind under the chignon, t his makes a striking head-dress, but gives the men an effeminate appearance.

I am here dealing only with personal adornments at ordinary times.

Unless they were under the influence of Europeans I never remember seeing a native, either male or female, with a clean head of hair. Their heads are always full of lice; it is quite common to see them going over each other's heads picking these out and cracking them with their teeth.

They never wash themselves, except when employed by whites, who then insist on them doing so. A wild native only requires water to quench his thirst. He only digs his gnamma-hole deep enough to dip a little water out, and barely a bucketful is exposed. There are many gnamma-holes all over the country. Some are permanent waters, more go dry.

When in mourning the women bedaub the whole person, hair and all, with white pipe-clay-the colour for mourning. The hair then hangs like white sausages. Widows always besmear themselves thus, and a fearful sight they look until it wears off, which takes many weeks. They cannot be persuaded to wash the pipe-clay off, or to swim in a waterhole, while it is on.

In hot weather the natives will swim in any water-hole. Although it is doubtful if the real sandhill blacks can swim, as there are no water holes in those parts deep enough, natives that come to the creeks and ranges as a rule can swim. Only by constantly reminding them will they even wash their faces and hands. A natural antipathy to cold water, as well as custom, prevents them from appreciating the benefits of cleanliness; which fact is regularly brought home to one when on their leeward side. At times, they shed a fragrance around which is simply overpowering. The native is fully alive to this. In hunting he carefully notes the direction of the wind, and runs it up, not down.

In addition to greasing and ochreing their bodies to make them shine (to "flash themselves" is the way they put it) the young men often wear the tail-feathers of the black cockatoo, which are black striped with yellow-red, or the white or yellow feathers of other varieties. The young women, for the same purpose, hang trinkets of kangaroo teeth set in spinifex resin from the hair or hang long necklaces of Stuart's beans several times around their necks, allowing them to hang down back and front as well. When in mourning they wear small bones dangling from the hair. The headband is universally worn, and is their most striking adornment. The dazzling white of it is from the white flour-like dust they gather from the bark of the so-called "limewood," a white stemmed variety of Eucalyptus (*E. papuana*). Both the white powder and the tree they call yt1lumba; sometimes *allumba.* They pierce the septum of the nose, and in it wear, as a rule, a quill, a bone, or piece of wood. The quill may have the tip of a rat's tail in the end of it.

Flowers are sometimes hung in the hair, or placed under the hairband, or even in the septum.

Both sexes pierce the septum of the nose and wear feather-quills therein.

As a rule natives whose country happens to be in or about the ranges are strong and healthy. I well remember a young fellow at Barrow Creek who made a typical Apollo; and another I saw on the Bonney possessed the most enviable symmetry of physique. The young women, too, have physical attractions; some have superb forms, and queenly gait. But they age quickly; their features and expression soon tell the tale of a hard life. In the matured woman, as a rule, the buttocks, hips, and upper thighs are large, while the lower thighs and calves are thin and bony. The shoulders and chests of the men are generally muscular and well developed, but from the elbows and knees to the extremities, the limbs, in most cases, have not the large muscles of the average European. The shoulders and arms of the women are bony and thin, as a rule.

I have never witnessed the actual incising of the cuts that form the skin decorations (cicatrices or keloids), the boring of the septum of the nose, or the knocking out of an incisor tooth. The two former operations are performed by male relatives when the boys and girls are twelve or thirteen years old. Both are regarded as improvements to the appearance, or presence, and the young people readily submit to the operations. The two first-mentioned practices are universal.

The knocking out of an incisor tooth was formerly very common, but not a universal custom. It seems to be regarded more as a ceremony, to distinguish the members of a clannish fraternity, than to make an improvement to the natural appearance. The practice has been hotly opposed by the whites from the start and, perhaps for that reason, appears to be dying out.

The custom of making fearful cuts across the thighs - some cut themselves over the shoulders - to mark their sorrow for a deceased relative, or to show sympathy for some untoward happening to a friend or relative, is evidently shared by all the tribes; few natives of middle age are without great scars that were self-inflicted for those reasons at some time or another. Cutting the thighs or shoulders is restricted to the men. The women's way, sometimes, for the same purpose is to gash the scalp with a sharp-edged or pointed stone; more often a pointed stick, such as a yam-stick, or a nulla-nulla, is raised upright above the head and brought down hard on the scalp until the blood flows freely, and streams down all over them. At such times they are a revolting sight.

The following incident, which occurred on my first journey from Barrow Creek to Victoria River, will show the peculiar mentality of the natives in regard to when, and for what, they should cut a great gash across the thigh to show their sorrow:

We had left the last-known water on the lower Hanson and were approaching what is now known as Circle Well. This was represented by our native guide to be the "first spring" (that is the way the guide put it) of several that he knew, and that would lead into the tract of country hitherto unexplored between Barrow Creek and Victoria River. So far as we knew it was a waterless stretch of over three hundred miles. Only Allan Davidson had crossed our projected route through the natives' "spring country." But the course he followed lay to the north of where the "springs" lay, and he had located no permanent waters.

For thirty miles out from the Hanson we crossed a gently undulating, sparsely timbered sandy tract, and then ran up against a formidable sand-dune, a veritable sand mountain. Up the side of this our guide led us in a slanting direction, as it was a formidable obstacle for the camels to scale. Presently we reached an elevation that overlooked a circular depression in the sand, partially open to the east, but bounded in all other directions by formidable sandhills. Our guide asked us to halt while he went and searched in the hollow for the "first spring." He had not visited the spot, he said, since he was a boy.

We espied a couple of natives out in the middle of the hollow; they did not see us, we being sheltered by low scrub. When our guide approached the spot where the natives were searching they caught sight of him; stared, then ran towards their camp Borne distance away. He called lustily to them to stop, and after much hallooing prevailed on them to halt while he explained the situation. They took him to the "spring" - a pool of water, perhaps three gallons in all, down in a broad-mouthed hole, under an overhanging rock, and six feet below the surface. We camped close to the "spring."

Later I asked our guide why the two natives ran away from him; they were his own people, and in his own country. He explained that, after looking him well over, they concluded that he had returned to them after long absence unaccompanied by even a friend - and destitute, as he carried neither spear, boomerang, nor shield.

Their sorrow for his sad plight was so great that they had resolved to show it by cutting a gash in their thighs. Had he not succeeded in stopping them before they reached their stone knives, they certainly would have done so.

13
POLYGAMY, POLYANDRY, AND MORAL MONSTROSITIES

AS a rule the young men possess only one wife. And she probably is quite an old woman; as his first wife a young man has apportioned to him some woman not coveted by middle-aged and older men. Since the advent of the whites, however, a young man will sometimes run off with a young woman. In former time either one or both of them would have been severely punished, very likely speared to death. The woman is usually an affianced wife - promised while very young by the parents to some suitor - although the man may not yet have taken her to him.

How the following rule was enacted is a mystery: A comparatively young man may sometimes become possessed of two wives by the death of an elder brother, the rule being that a younger brother receives the widow as a legacy, together with the children, if any. He may keep her for himself, or give her to some other man. The boy that got stabbed so badly for stealing another man's wife from Wycliffe Well (mentioned in the chapter "Punishments to Fit the Crime"), became possessed of a second wife and child through the death of an elder brother but he gave her to another man.

Strehlow states that a chief may have from three to ten wives. The rule is: When a man has a plurality of wives, those whom he does not require live in a separate camp; but they have to find him plant food and look after his children. They may, or may not, receive a little meat, or a bone thrown over his shoulder, by way of exchange. Let them commit any misdemeanours however, such as running away with another man (cases of which we have already cited) and they are likely to receive most brutal treatment. The women seem to be just as willing to elope as the men are to take them; they glory in it. Moat of the old men possess more than one wife, probably two, three, or four; a strong fighter may have five. Very seldom there are more than four.

Polyandry is not practised by the Aranda, nor so far as is known, by any tribe in Central Australia.

The vice of young men taking a youth about with them for immoral purposes has at times come under my notice. Strehlow states that there is no doubt that the custom obtains, not only among the Aranda, who have a definite word for the abominable custom, but also among all the tribes around. The two may travel about together for years.

The custom evidently receives the sanction of the old men, for the boy must belong to the marrying-class from which the man must select his wife; and the boy must not have gone through the initiation ceremonies that place him among the men. The reason, Strehlow thinks, may lie in the eight-class marriage system, which restricts the number of women available to him to narrow limits. Seeing how the old men monopolize the young women, by taking more than one, and up to ten, to wife, it is easy to see that a shortage of women is possible. Such shortage in tribes that have the four-class marrying-system would hardly be likely, and among those the custom is unknown, at any rate among the southern Aranda and Loritja tribes.

As a people, their morals are lax because they know no other way. They may be guilty of immodesty, but I would not call them immoral. Naturally they are concupiscent, but not vulgarly so. Almost without exception they are singularly free from coarse vulgarity. I have never seen what I would call a bold bad woman among them. Their speech before children is lewd and knows no restraint, but they see no necessity for hiding things that are always discussed with the utmost freedom.

I would not call them immoral because, from time immemorial, they have, through the sanction of the marriage code (presently to be explained) been in the habit of lending their women to other men. But the man must always belong to the lender's own class, the class the woman must select a husband from. As the lender always expects to receive some consideration in return, it is but a short step to lending the woman to some European in exchange for food and tobacco. I hold that the desire to acquire flour, tea, sugar, meat, and tobacco is the reason why native men send their women to the whites, or the women obtain permission to visit the Europeans' camps.

Food or tobacco is at the bottom of their indiscretions. Any project for the prevention of the intermingling of aboriginal and European strains to be successful must take this fact into account.

14
WOMEN'S HARD LOT

WHEN in the employ of Europeans and well fed the abnormalities of growing old early to a considerable extent disappear or do not develop; In their natural state native girls come to maturity early, and enjoy a short-lived time of youth and beauty. In a very few years the women grow wrinkled, bent, and old, miserable and discontented.

Evidently there is not much in the life of the elderly female native to be joyful about. It is one eternal round of toil; upon them rests the obligation of getting the major portion of the seeds and berries, lizards and snakes, and other edibles; as well as the grinding of the seeds and cooking. In times of drought, when all seeds are scarce or lacking, their lot is indeed a hard one. Children of both sexes, while out foraging, gather what food they can; but the drudgery falls on the women well up in years. And the parents here, as not seldom in more civilized communities, are often "sacrificed to the children."

When the season is bad, or if the woman has an objection to raising a child, she or the attendant woman sometimes destroys the child when first born. As a rule, however, they are fond of and indulgent to their children, and will give them the last bite of food. It is impossible to speak too favourably of the self-denying way in which the natives part with any little bit of food they may have to those in need of it.

Perhaps the most arduous work the women have to do is digging out yams. The memory of coming across yam-digging parties is still very vivid; the picture I see is like the following:

Diverse traverses are made through a sand-plain country that the women can reach from some fairly dependable water, not necessarily permanent. Later, you will run across a party of lubras digging for all they are worth. So intent will they be that they may not see you until you are right upon them, when they will emerge from three, four, or more holes, usually from four to six feet deep. The women will be without clothes, and will look for all the world as though they had been wallowing in a dust-heap, heads and all. By the holes you will see a clump of Eucalypt bushes that the tendrils of the climbing yam plant (*Ipomoea colobra*) lay hold of for support. You will be impressed with the labour yams cost to obtain.

Strehlow gives the following interesting particulars about the birth and disposal of children. Usually, when labour pains set in, a woman is taken by her near female relatives to a temporary shade and shelter, and there the delivery is assisted by pressing, or rough-massaging the lower parts of the body. After the birth is complete hot earth is placed on the body of the woman. The umbilical cord is severed by hitting it between two stones. The placenta is buried, but that part of the cord nearest the navel is dried, bound around with string, and then placed on the neck of the child, for good luck, and to promote rapid growth.

A new-born child is rubbed with soft well-beaten-up gum-tree bark, and is laid on a bed of the same in a wooden tray. In summer it is simply covered with a wooden tray, but in winter it is covered with bark like that on which it lies.

If twins should happen to be born, the elder (boy or girl) is regarded as a product of a *ratapa* (child-germ) that came in a westerly wind, and entered the mother through the hip or loins. As "bad-beings" come in westerly winds the child is therefore a west-wind bad-being child, and must be killed; so the grandmother hits it on the neck with a big stick and kills it straightway; or she may put a live coal or sand in its mouth to kill it, and the corpse she buries afterwards.

Strehlow suspects that the reason for killing one child of a twin-pair originated in the great effort a mother of twins has to make to carry two babies about when seeking for food. Sometimes both of the twins are killed. Should a child be born with an unusual development of hairs over its body, that also is an indication that it is a bad-being child.

A "not-wanted child" is sometimes killed by its mother or grandmother, by pressing her two thumbs into its stomach or (as in the example given below) by clasping the throat tightly with the hands.

The skin of a newly-born child is not dark brown, like that of a grown native, but light red in colour. In a few days' time it begins to darken, and in a month or two it assumes the normal colour.

The wooden troughs, or trays, in which the babies are carried are made from the extremely light and easily worked wood of Stuart's bean-tree, the foliage of which hangs down like a willow-tree; it affords a grateful shade to the traveller in a land where most of the trees throw a very poor shade.

Some days after its birth a child is placed in a tray on a bed of triturated bark, and taken to a spot near by. There a trench is dug, and dry kindling placed in the bottom of it. On this green twigs (of *Eremophila longifolia*) are spread. The kindling is fired, the mother of the child is called, and sits on the *Eremophila* twigs, and the mother and child inhale the fumes of the burning twigs as they rise around them.

The grandmother takes a twig in her hand and makes passes with it over the face and upper part of her daughter-in-law 's body, to increase the mother's milk-supply.

They then return to camp, and the mother-in-law cuts the mother's hair off with a stone knife, and singes the hair off the child with a small fire-stick. (If the long hair with which the child is born is allowed to grow the bad-being would come and eat up the child.) She also draws a coal-black stripe around the body, and over the face of the child, to ward off the bad-beings.

She also presses on the bridge of the child's nose to make it "handsome." The absence of a strong ridge to the nose, particularly just below the eyes, and the broad nostrils is a characteristic feature of the aborigines. These effects are apparently produced, at any rate to some extent, by exercising pressure on the nose in infancy. She also adorns the body of her daughter-in-law with red ochre.

During the time the mother remains in the women's camp after her accouchement her husband may see neither her nor the newly-born child, but he must provide her with meat for her sustenance. After, say, a week the child is laid on frayed bark in the tray and carried by the mother when she goes out to search for food.

If the child cries much she reminds it that its *tjurunga* is "lost," and that its father (grandfather) has gone to find it. If he finds it, that is, if it is made (for the supposed finding is a subterfuge only) and the binding it round and round with string so that no woman or child may see it is completed, it is then placed under the head of the child, under the bark in the tray. In that way it accompanies the child.

The *tjurunga*, or rather the benign influences it emits, is supposed to quieten and conduce to the growth of the child.

During this time the father usually makes a visit to friends in a distant camp, and returns home in a week or ten days' time, adorned with red ochre. After living for, say, a month in the women's camp the mother returns to her husband's camp and carries on her usual occupations.

I once asked a woman whom we had known to be enceinte what had become of her child. For answer she opened her two hands and encircled her neck and gave it a squeeze. She explained subsequently that it was not she that strangled the child as soon as it was born, but an old lubra with her at the time. The deed had been prearranged between them. The old woman also dug a hole and placed the dead child in it.

Another case of infanticide came under my notice.

It was in the early days, and the woman was known to be near her confinement, being one of the lubras that milked the cows at the Glen Helen station. One day she absented herself. It so happened that I travelled to the mission station on the following day. Upon arrival there the woman was there also. She had not only walked the twenty-odd miles in the time, but had given birth to a child, and dispatched it as well.

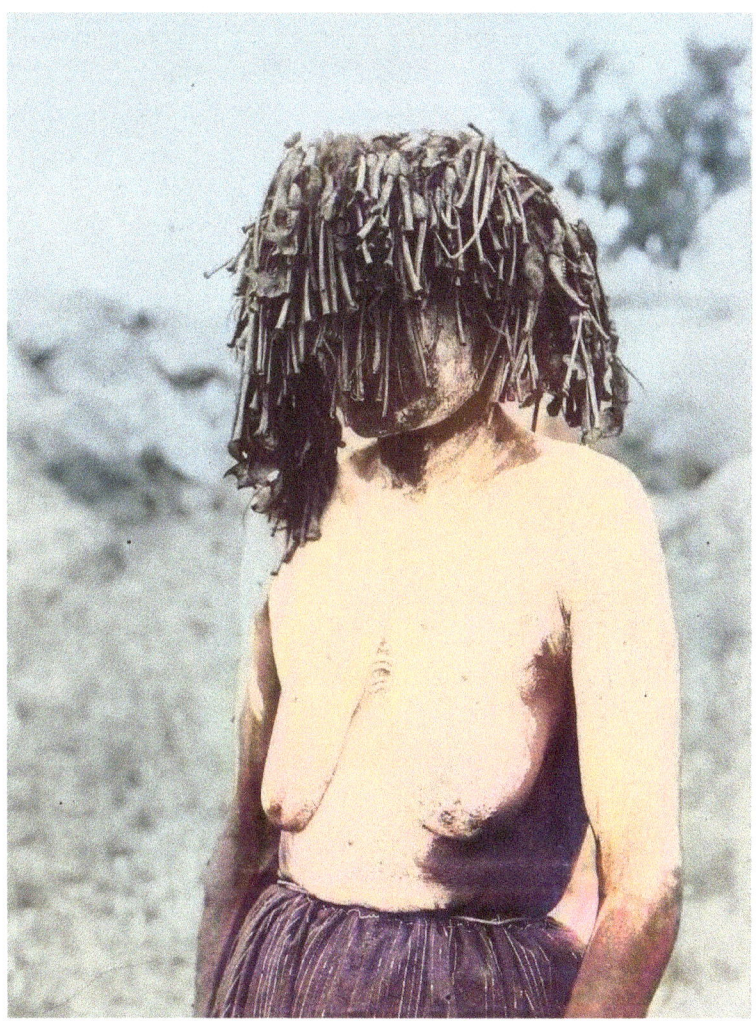

Aranda widow covered with pipe clay and wearing the *chimurilla* to scare the spirit of her husband away from the camp and into his grave.

15

EXPRESSIONS OF SORROW

THE sense of joy and sorrow, if not perhaps so lasting, is much the same in black as in white. I have seen strong men's as well as women's eyes rain with tears, and known that their cup of sorrow was full to the brim. Their conversation about departed ones is brief, and the words "death" or "dead" are spoken with bated breath; indeed they will resort to much circumlocution to avoid using either word. When one of their number is about to die they sometimes act in the most extraordinary way; and in some cases their sorrow is not always of the passive kind.

While I was camped at Connor Well a lubra (wife of one of the working boys) who had been ailing for a long time, died one afternoon. Knowing that the event was certain and imminent all the women and children gathered closely around her, and howled out their agony. The mourners grew more and more boisterous as the end drew near; covered the face of the invalid over with blankets, and crowded around as close as they possibly could, even pressing on the body.

At length the end came, but none knew when. As soon as the fact was discovered, fresh energy was put into their lamentations; all the men came and joined in as well. Their united efforts were easily heard at our camp, some distance away. I then walked across to witness the spectacle.

In anticipation a hole for the grave had been dug some half a mile or more away. The howling continued, each individual apparently vying with the others to see who could scream the loudest. This went on for perhaps a couple of hours when, without any observable sign, four men laid hold of the body, blankets and all, hoisted it on their shoulders, and rushed away with it as fast as they could go. A few followed; but the women sat where they were and continued to howl until well after dark. The wailing became intermittent throughout the night, and by morning had ceased, but it was revived each day at a stated hour, and sometimes in the night we heard it.

The form of burial in this case was to press the knees until close to the chin, and lay the body on its side in a niche dug out of the side, at the bottom of the grave. Twigs and leaves were placed against the niche opening to prevent the earth pressing on the body, and the grave was then filled in.

The situation and surroundings under which incidents occur add greatly to the impressions, transient or lasting, that they leave upon the memory. The following is one, nearly a quarter of a century old, that appears now as fresh as when it occurred. My party was sinking a well on a site we had already tested by boring. It was on the Hanson Creek north-west of the Barrow Creek Telegraph Station. As the sinking was not yet down to the water I, with a couple of black boys, took the camels to camp for three or four days at a claypan-water, also on the Hanson, but a few miles from where the well was being sunk.

At the claypans we found a camp of about thirty natives, men, women, and children. They were all bush natives. As always, I selected a fairly open spot in the shade of some trees to camp in; this had the advantage of a commanding view overlooking the natives' camps. They seemed to be unusually quiet.

No sooner were the camels let go than some of the native men came over and told me that one man was very ill, and asked for medicine to make him well. I immediately went over to see him. About fifteen natives, chiefly women, sat around the poor fellow. The near relatives sat next him, and tears filled their eyes, and ran down their cheeks. One held his head, but not in her lap, as they often do. He was very low, so low indeed that he might die any minute. I told them he would die very Boon; that I had left all my medicines at the well; and that, even if I had them, he was too far gone to take them.

Some two hours after I had returned to my camp a piercing cry rent the air, but it was not followed by the usual long-drawn-out lamentation that every one who has been in the neighbourhood of a native encampment when a death has occurred knows so well. Evidently the sick man had breathed again after the first cry had been uttered. We had not long to wait for a second cry, and soon the wailing became general. We were not near enough to see the wife (it was she who had rent the air with her cries) throw her body across the face of the dying man and the other women crowd on top of her. Probably many sick persons are suffocated in this way, children especially.

That wild, dreary, and terribly monotonous lamentation, "the belly moan," started then in earnest; and during my lonely three days' camp at the claypans it was so constant that I thought I must go mad. The belly moan breaks out suddenly, on a high note; then all the women join in unison and keep it up until tired out; it dies down, and quietness reigns for a while. Then suddenly some one of the women bursts out with the high note again, and all join in until the voices give out and there is another temporary suspension. Many times through the nights this occurred. It was terrible.

When I returned to the well the natives followed, and as water had been reached by that time they camped there and started on the belly moan again. It was a position that had to be faced. If they remained near my camp I should be crazy within a week, so I asked them as tenderly as I could to make their camp on the other side of the creek. They did so.

To return to the claypans. The man had not been dead more than two or three hours when about ten men rose quickly from where they had been talking some distance away. Very determinedly they hurried to the corpse, which was quite unclothed, hoisted it to their shoulders and walked as fast as they could to the grave - a hole three or four feet deep, with a niche in the side at the bottom, facing, so they said, "in the direction of the dead man's mother's mother's totem place; tba tis, where his grandmother received the *ratapa* (child-germ) that grew into his mother-in other words, conceived her." Strehlow has stated that to be the correct way. With knees pressed to the chin they laid the corpse on its side in the niche, face inwards (first cutting off its hair and beard); placed bushes against the body; scraped in the earth with their wooden *pittjis*, and heaped the earth up to a mound.

On the Finke they twist the dead man's hair into string.

I did not see the women tear their scalps with sharp sticks and stones, but their heads bore marks of such treatment later on. Neither did I see which men cut great gashes across their thighs, as is the custom in that part when a near relative dies. A few months previously I had seen two recent examples. The dead man had no' camp to burn at the claypans. All the natives shifted their camps to fresh situations; their superstitious dread of the man's ghost hovering around caused them to do this. The widow and the mother of the dead man bedaubed themselves, hair and all, with pipe-clay. Up to the time I left the locality not one of the natives could be induced to mention the dead man's name. Certain formalities as to relatives visiting the grave are practised in the Finke country, but I had no opportunity of seeing the in this case.

16

THE SIGN LANGUAGE

SIGN LANGUAGE has been developed to a remarkable degree by the Central Australian natives. I have had the fact deeply impressed upon me on very many occasions, and I doubt if the great length to which they have carried the art of conversing with one another on any subject of which they have cognizance is understood or appreciated to the extent it warrants. Both Spencer and Strehlow have recorded the meanings of some of the commonly used signs, but they .only touch the outermost edge of the art. Everyone with experience of the natives knows how well one native can express his wishes to another native as far off as he can see him plainly; but that is a small matter compared with carrying on a conversation, lasting for hours, on all sorts of subjects.

The natives have a custom they rigidly enforce, though it is barbarous in the extreme: that, upon the decease of certain relatives, women have a ban of silence for a given period, up to a year or more, inflicted upon them. It is then they acquire the highest stage of proficiency. There are few middle-aged women who have not gone through a twelve months' stretch without articulating a single word, and many of them have gone through two or three years of cumulative silence-bans.

During the ban-time they are permitted to make a mumbling sound to attract attention, but all communication and requests must be done by signs. All appear to understand the signs, but fluency in this silent conversation is only acquired by much practice.

Here are two or three very ordinary examples of how the sign language is practised: At the Francis Well one day I was watching a group of natives. An old woman, who could not speak a word of English, came and sat down among them. She did not speak a word, but made a certain sign with her hand which all assembled seemed to understand perfectly. I learned that she had seen a caravan of camels in the distance, and by a few signs had made known where the camels were, and to whom they belonged. On another occasion we were driving from the Taylor Crossing Well to Barrow Creek, and an old woman had seen fit to follow the van. It was a hot day, and the woman kept making signs to the boy in the van. On asking him what she was saying he gave us to understand that the old woman was begging him to ask us to stop and give her a drink of water or she would die.

There is no better way of finding out the true disposition of a person than to work with him, and the native is no exception. He soon throws off the mask of insincerity, and you see him as he is. Since my first acquaintance with the Central Australian natives, now fifty-five years ago, all have heard of white men, and all but a very few have seen them. Many have only seen them with some travelling caravan of explorers, prospectors or doggers.[8] Many wild natives who live far from European settlements have at some time or other journeyed in through some friendly tribes' country to some cattle, telegraph, or railway station, just to see what the white man really is like. These carry back to their friends vivid descriptions of railway trains, motor-cars and lorries, and, greatest wonder of all, the flying machines-all handled and worked by white men. Small wonder they like to come in and see for themselves.

17

THINGS THAT ARE PRIMITIVE

WE have discovered, but unfortunately far too late, that the natives are a very interesting people, with a primitive lore, a totemic belief and a social system peculiarly their own.

As regards former social cultures: they had no notion of fashioning clay into pottery. Their requisites for domestic use or defence purposes are made from wood, with stone knives, stone adzes, and stone tomahawks. Many quarries are known where they obtain stone, mostly diorite or dolerite, for tomahawks; and generally ¬quartzite or flint for knives. Certain men have gained reputations for being expert stone-knife manufacturers.

The stone knives used for performing surgical operations on the youths are small flakes of quartzite or flint.[9] Knives for general use vary in length from one to six inches. Many are hafted with spinifex resin only; some with wood and resin. The handle of a stone axe is a thin lath of green wood bent around the stone with the two ends lashed tightly together. These ends form the handle. The stick grips the stone tightly, but to keep it from shifting spinifex resin is melted with a fire-stick and pressed in all round. A chip of quartzite, fixed in the end of a spear-thrower that is gripped, serves for an adze for light work. For harder work it is fixed to a heavier short stick.

Of these implements only the stone portion is of lasting quality. All that one finds in the ancient camping-grounds are the above-mentioned axes, knives, and cutting-chips, and the millstones for grinding seeds for food. These latter are found near all the waters and principal camping-grounds. The deep grooves worn in the nether stones prove that they have done service through many generations. The sacred stone *tjurunga* are also durable, but they are found only in the store-houses.

There appears to be no evidence from any relics hitherto discovered in Central Australia suggesting more ancient cultures than that existing when whites first went among them. The tools the natives possess suffice to make the articles for their domestic needs, and for defence, under the present arid conditions; and there is nothing to show that they ever made, or possessed, any other kind of implements. Culturally these implements place the aborigines in the Stone Age. I prefer to leave it at that.

Every Central Australian native believes himself to be a direct descendant of some ancestor with attributes that far transcended the present status of human beings. They were not only supermen, but veritable gods with creative powers. If they wanted to be anywhere, neither rock, water, nor sky hindered their transit from place to place. They were there already. These ancestors lived upon the earth, and wandered up and down in it just as the natives do today. When they had done enough, they threw themselves on the ground and deliberately changed into a rock, a tree, a *tjurunga,* or some other natural object.

These natural objects, to the native mind, are neither emblems, tokens, nor symbols, but the real forefathers' bodies. So, when you look at, for example, the flat piece of stone or board, with a few crude designs scratched into it, that the native calls his *tjurunga,* you are gazing upon the ancestor himself. How absurd, you say. It is - from our point of view. But if you would understand. the native correctly, you must put yourself in his place and try to see things as he sees them. That is the way he regards those natural objects-rocks, trees, etc. - into which ancestors turned their bodies. These are scattered here and there allover the country, and are well known by the natives.

Again, the native believes that those natural objects are the homes of endless child-germs. And, being on the watch, if they espy a woman of the right class passing near, a child-germ leaves its home and enters the woman through the hip, loin, or navel to the uterus. There it germinates, and in due course a child is born. When he (the child) begins to talk he is told by his parents that he is a kangaroo, an emu, a duck, or some natural object. Then that particular creature or thing becomes his totem.

Apparently most of their immortal ancestors had a predilection for assuming the form of some particular animal or bird. To all intents and purposes they were those creatures. When tired out with the wear and tear of this life, they again changed; this time into rocks, trees, or *tjurunga,* from which child-germs of their particular kind could go out. If a forefather's adopted form was, say, that of an emu, then the rock he changed his. emu body into became the home of emu child-germs. If a woman received a child-germ while passing that rock her child of course might, and in all probability would, be a little emu. Her second experience might be while passing a kangaroo child-germ place, in which case her second child would be a kangaroo. The totem of the first child would be an emu; that of the second a kangaroo. In that way a native reckons he is the descendant of some particular ancestor; and explains why he belongs to some particular ancestor and totem. The mother and her totem don't count.

The other way whereby children originate is as follows; An ancestor throws a tiny *tjurunga* into a woman, where it immediately turns into a child-germ - the *tjurunga* being regarded as part of the ancestor.

Hence every native counts his descent from some totem-ancestor, whose totem of course he inherits.[10]

The totemic side of a native's constitution does not obtrude itself greatly when working among the natives, not nearly to the same extent that the Code or Class System does. Every one who has to do with the natives is confronted with the latter all the time. Totemic and class matters run side by side in the mind of a native; the two do not clash in any way. The Class System has to do with social and marriage customs; the Totem or Cult System is confined to a sort of religious worship, instructions, and ceremonial demonstrations.

The Class System, as already stated, pervades all the Central Australian tribes to the extent that a native belonging to a certain marrying-class must select his life partner from another specified marrying-class. The following diagram or code was drawn at Barrow Creek, and the names are those in use. It gives the key to the preceding and succeeding generations of both sexes.

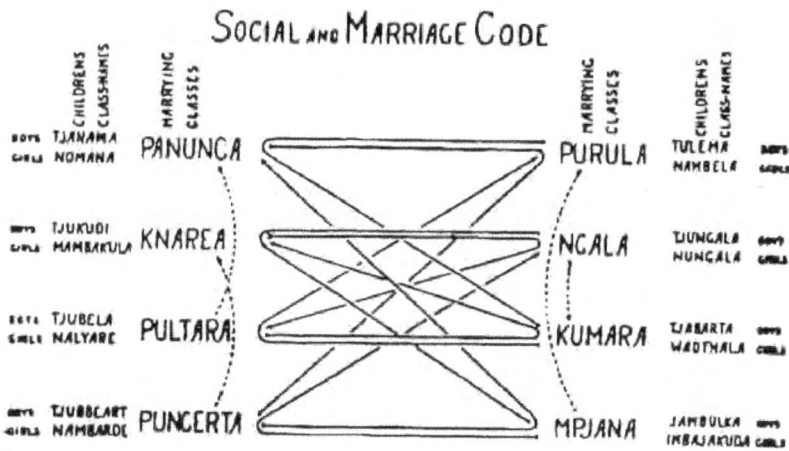

This diagram graphically shows the way the Central Australian natives' marrying-system works. The butts of the arrows indicate the men in that class who may marry the women in the class opposite (indicated by the bend in the shaft) and the point indicates the class into which the children of that union, both male and female, past; and their class-name. By following the arrows forward, one after the other, the paternal descendants can be readily traced. By following them backwards a man's antecedents can also be readily found. In the same way by using the bends (representing the women) in the shafts as starting-points the maternal descendants or antecedents, as the case may be, are clearly seen. The dot-and-dash arrows indicate classes that are strongly taboo to each other.

The system is essentially a class system of marriage.

If it were not that the natives have a very clear idea of blood relationships, and are averse to marriages of that sort or contracts between the very young to that end, the system might defeat the object for which it appears to have been created. In practice the grandchildren of brothers and sisters marry each other, which means that a man has to marry his second cousin, and the children (male and female) of the union automatically pass into, their father's father's (paternal grandfather's) class. The result of this is that a man's children go into his father's class, and not into his wife's father's class. The class line of descent is therefore in the paternal line among the tribes that we this code. Probably, before the whites disarranged things, the union of second cousins (class. cousins) contained no blood affinity whatever.

It is really astonishing to find in communities so backward that all the people are so well versed in the routine working of the marriage code: Every native is conversant with its details. No precepts were ever taught to a nation more thoroughly. The teaching commences in infancy. As soon as it can lisp a word every child is taught its class-name - the name shown in the diagram, which corresponds to the class into which it passed when born.

Every native knows he must not select a wife from his own side (moiety) for the following reasons:

(a) In one of the classes all the women are taboo, for they are all mothers-in-law to him;

(b) In another class the women are all first cousins to him;

(c) The remaining class holds his children; that is, it is his children's grandparents' class.

All the children of his own children's generation, no matter who begot them, he calls his children. In this way a man has scores of children, scores of fathers, and mothers, and aunts and uncles.

Furthermore, the natives have a specific name for every relationship.

In the Totem System there is a sort of brotherhood between those who are of the same totem. In the Class System the bond of friendship between those persons belonging to a particular class is more pronounced. One of the first questions that strangers ask of one another when they meet is: What is your class? If it is the same as the questioner, he is accepted as a brother Mason; and, if any food is about, he will be given some. In everyday contact with the natives one notices that the Class System is very much more in evidence than the Totem System. One may not discover the totem of a native working for one for some time; perhaps never, unless one asks specially for it; but one of the first things one gets to know is his or her class. A man or woman is often addressed by his or her class-name.

Every child is given (is actually born with) a class-name that corresponds to its class (see the diagrams) which "child's name" often sticks until middle life is reached, or longer. All the boys in the same class bear the same name; so with all the girls.

When one has mastered the practical working of the diagram the mention of a boy's name enables one to avoid the inconvenience often occasioned by the engaging of natives who have to work together but are taboo to one another. You have his name, say, Tjabbarta; you then know that he belongs to the *Kumara* class; that his mother is a *Panunga*, and his father a *Purula*. You also know that if you have a *Ngala* woman in your employ that she is taboo to him, for she is his mother-in-law (one of scores), and that you will not be able to get him to go near her, or vice versa. So you promptly down his application for a job, because of that.

I have had many years' experience in working the natives, and this is the result: Of all the tribulations one suffers in trying to work men and women of taboo classes, none equals the trouble caused by the "strong taboos." The only way to avoid endless friction is to select a gang in which the following relationships are not present:

(a) A woman and her mother-in-law's brothers; for a woman's mother-in-law's brothers are prohibited from looking at, going near to, or speaking to her, and vice versa;

(b) A man and his mother-in-law and her sisters; for a man's mother-in-law and her sisters are prohibited from looking at, going near to, or speaking to him, and vice versa.

The situation can only be fully appreciated by remembering that all the women in that mother-in-law's class bear the same relation to him- they are all mothers-in-law, scores and scores of them.

Marriages that conform to the code are called "straight marriages"; any divergences from it are called "crooked marriages." As already stated, each pair of "straight" intermarrying classes are "second cousins'" to one another. The first pair (keeping on the horizontal lines of the code) are first cousins to the second pair, and vice versa; as also are the third pair to the fourth, and vice versa. The second and third pairs are different - parents and children being the relationship in that case.

Before the influence of the whites obtruded itself the marriage code undoubtedly was much more rigorously enforced. As a result we have today "crooked marriages," and "crying scandals of marriages" that must horrify the elders. The, following glaring instances came under my notice:

(a) A man marrying his niece;
(b) A man marrying his maternal grandmother; [11]
(c) Several cases of second cousins marrying first cousins;
(d) A woman, well known at Barrow Creek, who wished to marry her (class) son. Ridicule, and pressure from the other women made her relinquish that infatuation after some months of trial marriage with him. Then she married her (class) father.

The children of "crooked marriages," as also their parents, are subjects of ridicule. When this happens the parents try to get their children called by the names they would have borne had the marriage been a "straight" one; much social scheming is resorted to to gain that end.

Some minor taboos are often noticeable; they savour of etiquette to some extent. Strehlow mentions the following: A woman may visit her father's camp during his absence. Upon his return he may not enter his camp, but he can speak with her at a distance. When he is in camp she may come near enough to talk to him, but she may not enter his camp while he is in it. The same rule applies to all the men in her father's class; they (with the solitary exception of her own father) are all (class) fathers to her. Similar rules apply in regard to her grandfather's camp. A man may come reasonably close to his paternal aunts. A man may go to his mother's camp at any time. It may here be mentioned that the elderly females, not-withstanding that they are abject slaves to their spouses, wield a powerful influence over the young ones. They are "sticklers" for society rules; more especially while their husbands are onlookers.

There are many other minor taboos.

After puberty there is always a degree of reserve and shyness between the sexes, whether well acquainted or not; both sexes make wide detours when they have to pass a group, or a camp, of the opposite sex. A man wishing to give food to a woman that is taboo to him takes it to a place she can see, but keeps his eyes off her the meanwhile. He makes some noise to attract her attention, and retires. She then gets the food. When both have to get water at the same place one hangs back until the other has taken water and gone. It is considered bad form for either sex to "presume" and be too friendly with the opposite sex when they belong to the parents' or grandparents' generation.[12] It amounts to a mild taboo. Brothers and sisters can speak to one another unreservedly, as also can second cousins. First cousins, on the other hand, can speak to one another, but they can't go to a man's camp like second cousins. A man can speak to his maternal grandmother at a distance. Much visiting goes on between the women in the daytime; they con-gregate under a shady tree, and spend hours in gossiping. The men do likewise. When night approaches they file off to their own camps.

As regards the code itself: When expressed diagraphically the completeness of it becomes apparent at once. The whole scheme suggests gradual growth:

(a) Promiscuous marital rights as with animals;

(b) Then a communism as regards marital rights between the two communities (moieties) into which the people were probably divided;

(c) Next, in course of ages, each moiety was divided into two classes, and marital rights were restricted to only one of the two classes in the opposite moiety. That obtains today in tribes that lie farther south;

(d) Finally, at a much later date, the two classes in each moiety were again divided - making four marrying-classes in each - and marital rights were further restricted to one only of the four classes in the opposite moiety.

Probably at the third stage the relegating of the children to certain classes was first instituted. And at the fourth the problem of where to place the children was solved. That they succeeded so well in devising a cleverly designed, complicated, and yet very smooth-running code, does them great credit.

Communism, theoretically, and to a large extent practically, still obtains as regards the reciprocating marrying-classes, for all the women are regarded as possible wives, and all the men as possible husbands; and between them marital relations are permissible-unless someone has obtained prior rights over the woman. But the communistic principles have been perverted by the old men. Instead, they have practised "the good old rule, the simple plan, that he shall take [of the women] who has the power, and he shall keep who can." Hence we find that some men possess several wives while others cannot get one.

An Arrernte emu man, performing the sacred totem of his group. Alice Springs, 1896.

18

WHAT OF THEIR FUTURE

WHAT is in store for the sixty thousand or so aborigines in Australia ~ Can a people so backward withstand for long the impact, and compete successfully in the battle of life with Europeans? If not, what is to become of them? If one may judge from the rapid decrease in their numbers since the advent of white people in Australia, they are destined to complete extinction not many generations hence. Unfortunately that has already come to pass in Tasmania. Only within recent years have their unique characteristics been fully appreciated, and with that knowledge has come the shock that whole tribes have gone; and that what they could have told us is lost forever.

Lack of knowledge and experience, more than want of heart, probably, is the reason why they were neglected, for they have always had many sympathizers. Great credit is due to the pioneers and station-people generally. Besides supplying the natives with food and clothes, they trained them to be useful. Had they not done so their lot would have been bard indeed. Regrettable incidents have occurred, but the kindness shown to the natives by the pioneer settlers far outweighs any injustice they did them. The blame for those indiscretions rightly belongs elsewhere.

It is a healthy sign that schemes for the betterment of the natives are eagerly read by thoughtful Australians. Advocates of new ideas are many, but their individual efforts usually result in transient notoriety, nothing more, owing to their lack of practical experience of the natives. No-one can be clear and constructive unless he has thorough knowledge of his subject, and for that reason before any radical change is made the pioneer settlers in any district concerned should always be consulted.

Scientists are giving our aborigines very great attention; studying their language and lore, measuring them, taking plaster casts, movie photos and cinematograph records of them in their daily occupations; but much valuable information has been lost owing to whole tribes in the south-eastern quadrant of Australia having already become extinct. In a few years we shall have gathered together much valuable information about the remainder. But the scientist is insatiable. He wants the uncontaminated natives kept in their primitive state mentally, morally, and in every other way, so that they can be further studied. He has pleaded successfully for large reserves, and would keep them there as zoological curiosities.

Missionaries and their supporters see in these huge reserves some hope of establishing mission stations there, of keeping the natives within the within the reserved boundaries, and of bringing about in them a complete transformation from barbarism to civilization, from totemism to Christianity. The material the missionaries have to work on is more obtuse than refractory, and as their authority over the natives is restricted to suasion the headway can only be slow. However, the objective is a laudable one, and their humanizing influence cannot be other than for good.

Mission stations make useful ethnological stations. From Pastor Schulze came the first intelligent account of the Central Australian natives. Kempe produced the first grammar; and both the first vocabulary of the Aranda language. The monumental work of Strehlow is referred to many times in these pages. From the ethnological standpoint Hermannaburg, on the Finke, has justified its existence many times over.

The general public care little for the scientific aspect, and less for the natives' religious beliefs; but they do want to be assured that the natives receive just and kindly treatment; that they be allowed to come and go when and where they please and to work for whom they please. They insist that proper official surveillance be kept over the natives to see that they are not imposed upon by unscrupulous persons; that they do not kill one another, or menace the whites in any way. In short, they must conform to our laws, and keep the peace.

The general public think that, as the natives' land, or part of it, is now run over by stock, the former food supplies considerably reduced thereby, and game scared from the natural waters, the aged and sick should be fed; that all who are able to work, or hunt, be required to do so; that medical attendance be compulsory and free; that capable advocates should be supplied to those apprehended in court; that small reserves adjacent to white settlements if not already declared, should be apportioned to them, as well as specified camping grounds.

There is still another, and what may be called "the extremist section," who seem to think that every white man in the bush is a human monster; that he has done nothing but exploit and pollute the blacks from the start, and consequently the blacks must be yarded off in some compound where his baneful influence can never again reach them. They never fail to bring as evidence some ancient tale of the barbarities that were alleged to have been perpetrated on the blacks, the more gruesome the better.

Let us examine how far the natives are likely to respond to the big reserves and complete isolation idea. Every station owner in the interior knows that the natives have been drifting in from far outback for the last fifty years.

Mrs Daisy Bates has stated again and again that the natives come in to the Ooldea Railway Station from great distances, Pastor F. W. Albrecht, Strehlow's successor at the Finke Mission Station, in a letter in the public press some time since, made special reference to the way the natives from far outback come into the Finke Mission Station. He says:

> They are drifting in because the white man's teaching is shaking their religious beliefs, and undermining their social organisation. Their unbounded faith in magic is being shattered by the ridicule that the whites pour into them. The native has arrived at the stage when he willingly parts with his most sacred *tjurunga* and other ceremonial objects to the whites for a little tea or sugar, flour or clothing, and having done so means the end of his old beliefs and of ever reviving them again.
>
> In his natural state he has to fight his enemies, and also work hard, and all the time, for his living. He also has demons to fight, in which conflict he reposes his trust in magic, and they have now become uncertain, having disposed of their sacred objects, of the end of the conflict, feel inferior, and fear creeps into them that eventually will drive them away from their old haunts, to the white man to seek protection and a substitute for what they have lost. It would make very sorry reading if the real story of the wandering native should be written. The Stone Age man stands in jeopardy of being swallowed up by twentieth century civilization. *It is certain that, even if it were tried, no policing of them to keep them back in their own country would keep them there. The impact with the white is inevitable sooner or later, and only kindness and protection can postpone for a little the time when their complete extinction will have to be recorded.*

I have already written of their avenging habit. A heavy mortality results from these murderous excursions. The slaughter of children also accounts for a good many lives. Infectious and contagious diseases decimate their numbers. An epidemic of flu that ran through the interior a few years ago wiped out a great many. In some instances they were so terrified that they abandoned and fled from the sick ones as if they had been stricken with the plague. Venereal disease is rampant. That the scourge was introduced by the whites is not yet proven. Strehlow's inquiries revealed that they were afflicted with it before the whites came. Pulmonary affections carry off a number every year. The pitted skin on some shows that smallpox has been among them. Lack of food in severe droughts accounts for the aged, the infirm, and some of the very young.

> If the native earns and is given money he squanders it. He is woefully deficient in business acumen; indeed he has not the slightest aptitude for spending judiciously, for dealing or striking a bargain, or for

making provision for the food he knows he will need on the morrow. He has not arrived at that stage in civilization. Nature hitherto has provided sufficient food for his sustenance, and consequently the necessity for making provision jor the future is foreign to him.

Having always lived in a communistic atmosphere he has no sense of value. A sixpence is as good as a shilling. If a man, a woman, or a boy is given a "rig out" of clothes, it will be given to someone else tomorrow, perhaps in exchange for some old dirty rag. They will gamble at cards or on the spin of a coin for the shirts on their backs.

Someone must think and act for them, to see that they receive the necessaries of life, and that unscrupulous persons, white or black, do not defraud them of their portion. They think the whites can do anything; that money and food and clothes flow to us naturally, with little effort; and that therefore the whites have unlimited quantities to give away.

The natives are very partial to the white man's food, and the white population in the interior is always giving away food and clothing to the natives that rightly belong to that spot. That induces strange natives to hang around stations, townships, railway camps, and so forth. Many come from parts hundreds of miles distant. Some journey to the whites' settlement through curiosity, and some to get employment. Others, as Albrecht states, come in for protection from retribution that awaits them for having offended tribal laws. Food, however, is the main thing they are after. It is so much easier to get food, either from the whites themselves - for all participate when a beast is slaughtered - or from natives in work.

This drifting in of the outback natives will effectually prevent their permanent retention in the mammoth reserves that have been declared, and dooms the idea of preserving them in their future state" to failure, even before it has a trial. It is a setback also to the advocates of shutting the natives off entirely from the "wicked whites" whose touch they believe contaminates them. This panacea evidently had its birth in dreamland, for no person with any practical knowledge of the natives believes that they can be retained within a given area without strongly policing them. And the cost of that would be prohibitive.

It may be that the area in which it is desired to retain them, is their own country. But who is to say that they shall not travel beyond the bounds of their own country? And beyond the reserve also? It should never be forgotten that the natives are nomads, and were born with the nomadic instinct in them; their traditions state that their totem-ancestors were nomads, and they have been nomads ever since. That being so, to restrict their liberty in any way would be a cruel wrong. They love their own country, but that does not damp the desire in them to see more distant parts. When the desire to wander takes them they *must* go.

Reserves are useless for natives whose country lies beyond the boundaries. If a native from some other part desired to make his home there he would probably be told to stay in his own country, as he would eat the food that belonged to other natives. Or it may be that some old grudge remains still outstanding, in which case if he went there unprotected by a white man the chances are be would be speared to death. Reserves are useless unless. they are under a white man's supervision.

And unless the natives within them are kept under strict police surveillance they are likely at any time to menace the lives of either black or white people. The murdering of whites as well as people of their own colour that occurs so often shows that the natives must be taught to obey the white man's laws. They must be taught not to kill one another, and to respect the rights of others. I would let them retain their totem-ancestor creed; practise their initiation rites on the lads; and their own marriage code. But there must be no compulsion: that is, if a lad could not be induced by suasion to undergo the ceremonies it would be illegal to take him by force; and illegal to force a girl to marry against her wish. If, as Albrecht states, their religious props are being ruthlessly knocked from under them by ridicule, it may be possible to substitute a creed of superior moral value, and of more immediate benefit to them, by teaching them how by work to earn their living, and to be thrifty and clean.

They are shot through with magic; and magic in some form or other is at the bottom of most of the crimes. The innocence or guilt of a culprit is mostly decided by magic; consequently it is essential that something more tangible· should replace their belief in magic. Albrecht has, perhaps unknowingly, mentioned the only way, probably, by which their faith in magic may be undermined - by ridiculing such beliefs. That can only be effected by close contact with the whites. The working boys, for example, often get their belief in magic shattered in that way.

That belief is a serious matter, and lies at the root of the great question the Federal Government is up against: Is the Government policy regarding the native question to be an attempt at keeping them in their present backward state, and isolated from the whites? Or are they to be brought into still closer contact with and given the full benefit of association with the whites; given facilities and encouragements to improve themselves; made law-abiding; taught how to become useful citizens and earn their own living?

Assailed from all sides by the advocates of multifarious ideas the Government has probably not yet devised a clean-cut policy. One thing is certain: the natives in different parts of the continent require very different methods of treatment. That is only to be expected, because of the very diversified conditions under which they live.

In his natural state the native of the centre has to work hard to get a living. That keeps him mentally alert and physically fit. If removed from his own hunting-grounds he is stranded, for those grounds are his in a very special sense; and pining for them, he will return sooner or later if he gets a chance.

Then again: If his food and clothes are supplied him without making him exert himself as he has been accustomed to do, or if he is allowed to sponge on the working boys indefinitely, he either gets up to some mischief or degenerates into a lazy, useless being, and soon dies of ennui. Hence it is essential that he should remain in his own country, if he is not a working boy, and be found some occupation, so that he may work out the value of the food he eats and the clothes he wears - if possible before he gets them. Nothing is so bad for the native as to feed him in idleness. As soon as he loses the incentive to work he goes downhill.

Where the country is leased and stocked with sheep or cattle, natives whose country lies there have in large part lost their living; the stock drink from the natural waters, and frighten the game away. In such cases the Government is under the moral obligation to make good the deficiency of food thus caused.

Fortunately the art of tending stock, transporting stores, and other occupations are soon learned by the younger generations, who are thereby absorbed; but the parents of the workers, being too old and obtuse to learn, cannot be so employed. They can, however, find in the bush most of the food they require. The old and infirm, and the blind, are fed by the Government if they live near the food-distribution stations. The pastoral stations of course find employment, food and clothing for most of the workers and their relatives, and to them belongs the chief' credit of training the natives to be useful.

Personal contact with the whites, I repeat, produces a human being on altogether a different plane to the warrigals, who are really a Stone Age product. No better examples can be found of the civilizing effect of personal contact with the whites than the working native boys and women; and no other equally successful method has yet been devised to improve the natives as properly regulated personal contact with the respectable white man.

The gradual and mysterious disappearance of whole family groups, until not one remains - not-withstanding that they were well cared for - is a mystery, but a fact all the same. All that we know is that they started to die as soon as the whites came among them. A case in point was the tribe that occupied the Ulooloo Creek country, where I was born, and spent my early years. The natives there received great kindness at the hands of the settlers, but they just faded away one after the other until all were gone. The same thing appears to be taking place wherever the whites occupy the country in numbers. As stated above, the natives come to the whites' settlements from far and near, and having once tasted the white man's food they are not to be denied coming again. The younger members seek employment, and thereby become transformed out of all recognition. But the older men and women never change. Nothing can be done to improve them, and their passing should be made as pleasant as circumstances will permit.

There is some hope for the younger generation of both sexes if taken in hand early, treated kindly but firmly, and disciplined in some useful occupation. They need to be lifted out of their naturally squalid habits of living. By adopting the white man's ways they may overcome the tendency to "die out," for those in work are healthy enough.

What now follows, although not strictly within our subject, lies on the borderland and may be of interest:

As is the case the wide world over where there is great disparity in the sexes of the white population living among black races, there are half-castes in Central Australia. A result that should have been foreseen, and doubtless will continue while the disparity lasts. The cross is much more stable than the black. The number of half-castes, quadroons, and octoroons is increasing, and giving the authorities concern. One of the saddest remembrances the writer retains of the Finke was of a young half-caste woman of prepossessing appearance living in the blacks' camp, with a blackfellow as husband. The missionaries it was said had married them. The Federal Government has now forbidden such unions; half-castes must marry whites and breed the black out, or as commonly expressed "breed them white."

The future of the Central Australian natives lies in the lap of the gods. All experience points to the race becoming extinct within a few generations, The one hope of prolonging their existence seems to lie in the direction of improving the race by means of teaching and especially by personal contact with reputable white people.

NOTES

1. Gnamma: to dig. Gnamma-hole: & dug-out hole.
2. See a paper by Professor Cleland and Johnson in the *Proceedings of the Royal Society of South Africa,* vol. lvii, pp. 113·24.
3 Cleland and Johnston think *N. Gossel.*
4 All natives employed in the service of the whites, irrespective of age, are called "boys.
5 The well is fifty miles south of Alice Springs.
6 *ilbo:* the uterus; *manl:* not barren.
7 *alkna:* eyes; *rintja*: turned away.
8. Men who poison or trap dogs tor their scalps. They travel far outback and live for months at a stretch among the natives. They enlist the help of the natives in catching the dogs.
9. Glass is preferred in these later times.
10. For this explanation of native genealogy I am largely indebted to Strehlow.
11. This was regarded as a heinous offence, for the woman belonged to "his own side" (or moiety). Being the shepherd at Barrow Creek the man had, of course, the protection of the whites. He was also a redoubtable fighter. But he always went in fear that the other natives might murder him.
12. The murder of Bendigo, related in Chapter 8, is an instance of how strongly the natives resent undue familiarlty.

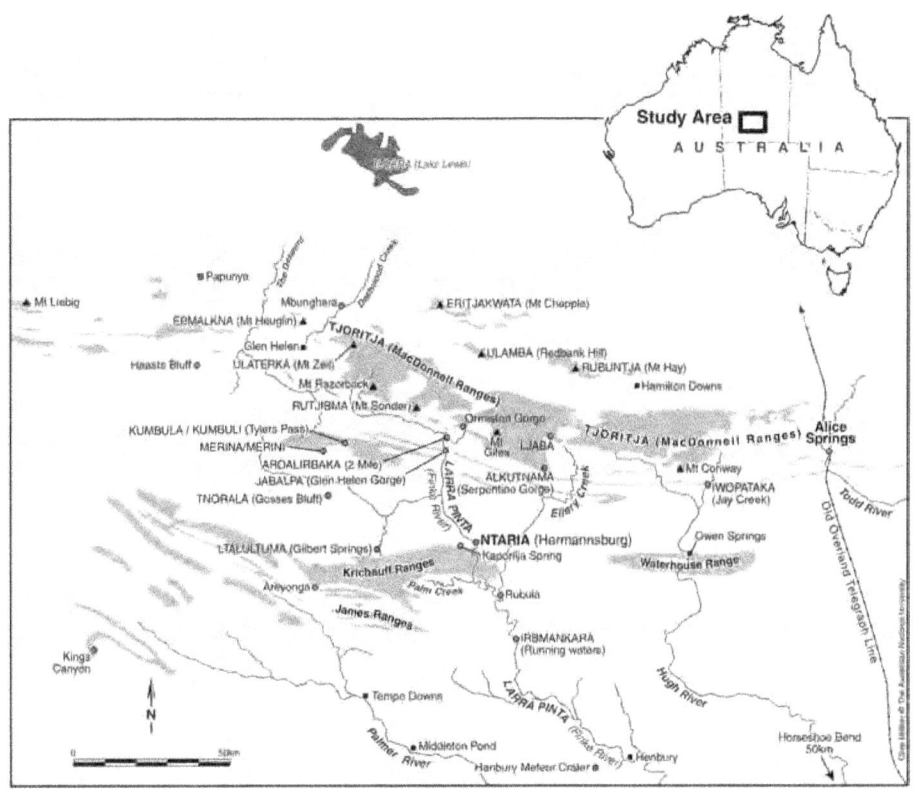

Map of Alice Springs and surrounds prepared by Chris Hillier for the Australian National University.

www.ingramcontent.com/pod-product-compliance
Lightning Source LLC
Chambersburg PA
CBHW042141160426
43201CB00021B/2362